Joseph Joffo

# Un sac de billes

## and other writings

Tony Simons

Lecturer in French Studies
University of Reading

UNIVERSITY OF GLASGOW
FRENCH AND GERMAN PUBLICATIONS
2004

University of Glasgow French and German Publications

Series Editors: Mark G. Ward (German)
Geoff Woollen (French)

Modern Languages Building, University of Glasgow,
Glasgow G12 8QL, Scotland

First published 2002; reprinted 2004.

Printed by KKS Printing, London E9 6JE.

ISBN 0 85261 696 1

# Contents

# Citations and editions

*Un sac de billes* was originally brought out by Jean-Claude Lattès in 1973, and it is in the publishing house's subsequent paperback edition (1997) that the starting date of 1942, not 1941, is given. The work has since appeared in many budget-priced editions, frequently children's. Of these, the Livre de Poche 'Jeunesse' of 1998 contains information about Joffo, the historical context, and a thematic dossier designed to encourage critical appreciation, while the one of 1982 contains (pp. 375-82) an important essay by Fred Kupferman. A significant consultation problem is that of different paginations; bracketed page references given in **bold** typeface, e.g. (**38-41**), are to the Livre de Poche first published along with Joffo's 'Dialogue avec mes lecteurs' in 1992, and most recently in 2000.

*Baby-foot*, originally published by Jean-Claude Lattès in 1977, has had a similar history, with the result that pagination again is not consistent. Bracketed page references, given in plain typeface, e.g. (39), are to the Livre de Poche edition of 2001.

The 'prequel', *Agates et calots*, written by Joffo to satisfy public demand, was published by Éditions Ramsay in 1997, and by Le Livre de Poche in 1998. Page references, e.g. (p. 7), are to the latter.

P.A. Brooke's edition of *Un sac de billes* (London: Routledge, 'Twentieth-Century Texts', 2000 [1989] ) contains an introduction, notes and bibliography of source material, but not the 'Dialogue avec mes lecteurs'.

Martin Sokolinsky's translation, *A Bag of Marbles* (University of Chicago Press, 2000 [1974]), has made a welcome reappearance.

Critical works listed in the bibliography are all numbered, and when reference is made to them in the text, indicated between brackets with the figure denoting them in italics, followed by the page number(s), e.g. (*13*, pp. 14-15).

# Chronology of key events

1789      The French Revolution leads to the setting up of the French Republic, the introduction of the national motto 'Liberté, Égalité, Fraternité' and the Déclaration des droits de l'homme.

1870-1871      The Franco-Prussian War leads to France losing Alsace-Lorraine.

1897-1899      The main years of the Dreyfus Affair: a wave of popular nationalism and anti-Semitism in France.

1914-1918      World War One, in which Marshal Philippe Pétain is acclaimed as a hero for the French, winning the Battle of Verdun in 1916. The 1919 Treaty of Versailles gives Alsace-Lorraine back to France.

1924      Adolf Hitler writes *Mein Kampf*, in which he expounds his theories on racial purity and a new European Order.

1926      The Nazi Party creates the SS, its military wing.

1933      Hitler becomes Chancellor of Germany; the Nazi Party becomes the only party in Germany; the Gestapo (political police) is set up; the first concentration camps including Dachau are created. In Dachau, the first inmates are political prisoners but eventually about one third of the prisoners there are Jews.

1936-1938      Léon Blum leads the coalition Front populaire ('front popu' [208]) government to power in France. It is left-wing, firmly republican, anti-fascist and anti-Nazi.

1938      Germany annexes Austria. In October, the Munich Agreement—signed by Chamberlain for Britain, Daladier for France, Hitler for Germany and Mussolini for Italy—exchanges the Sudetenland (the

German-speaking territory in the north of the Czech Republic) for a promise by Hitler that he would end his expansionist policies.

1939    German-Soviet Pact; Germany invades Poland; Britain enters the war to support Poland; the 'drôle de guerre' begins in France.

1940    Germany invades France in May. A massive exodus of the population ensues, with millions of civilians leaving their homes; 18 June, de Gaulle makes his famous speech from London, calling on the French to resist; on 22 June, the French government led by Marshal Pétain signs an armistice effectively dividing France into two parts, an Occupied Zone comprising the northern and western parts of the country, and an Unoccupied Zone comprising the south-eastern part; Pétain is given full powers in the Unoccupied Zone, with his government based at Vichy; announcement by Pétain of a 'Révolution Nationale', leading to a change from 'Liberté, Égalité, Fraternité' to 'Travail, Famille, Patrie', and to the introduction of the first measures restricting the rights of Jews in both the Occupied and Unoccupied Zones; in August 1940, Alsace-Lorraine is annexed by Germany.

1941    The round-up of Jews begins.

1942    In July, with the help of the French police, approximately twelve thousand men, women and children are arrested, gathered at the *Vel'd'Hiv*, sent to concentration camps such as Drancy and then to extermination camps in Germany.

1943    Nice is occupied by the Italians from November 1942 to September 1943; Germany's campaign in Russia fails at Stalingrad.

1944    The Liberation of France; de Gaulle heads a provisional government in Paris.

# Introduction

At the end of *Un sac de billes,* in his 'Dialogue avec mes lecteurs', Joffo recounts a story telling how a group of children, playing at marbles in a school playground, were heard to insult other children as 'Youpins' and 'Sale juif'. In response to the telling-off by the headteacher, one of the children replies: «Monsieur... C'est pour rire. On joue à Joffo... Au *Sac de billes*» (**253**).

The headteacher tells Joffo in amazement that the children hurling the insults were themselves Jewish and the others not, and asks Joffo what he thinks of the incident. Joffo comments that, through play, people can try out roles that they would not be able to adopt in real life, experiencing what they could never experience in reality. He adds that such an exchange of roles is inevitably false, since the real situation can never be recreated. He completes his commentary more equivocally:

> Mais j'ajouterai ceci, qui me paraît le plus important: je n'étais pas mécontent de voir mon aventure devenue un jeu d'enfants. Je serais encore plus heureux qu'elle le reste, et que les adultes, eux, n'aient plus jamais envie d'y jouer. (**253**)

The levels of reflection in these final statements of the 'Dialogue avec mes lecteurs' go to the heart of Joffo's works. There is always a commitment to the shared understanding of the nature of Jewishness, whatever the context and whatever the genre. Even in his non-autobiographical works, there is always a personal commitment, a sense of involvement in his own life and its events, and there is always a strong sense of didacticism, of underpinning his writing with a message. That this message is linked to harmless play or to tragic reality, or both at once, is one of the fascinations of his work.

Joffo started writing during enforced recuperation following a skiing accident in 1971. His works encompass a wide range of themes, but the most significant common ones are those of the Jewish experience and of childhood. He deals with these in an autobiographical way in *Un sac de billes* (1973), its sequel *Baby-foot* (1977), and the 'prequel' *Agates et calots* (1997). Between the first two came *Anna et son orchestre* (1975), which recounts how his mother and grandmother escaped the pogroms in Odessa during the Civil War of 1918-1921 that broke out after the Bolshevik Revolution in Russia.

Many of Joffo's most popular works such as *Un sac de billes* appeal particularly to children, and he also published in 1980 two short works especially for children, *Le Fruit à mille saveurs* and *La Carpe*. However, they also have an adult audience, adults being able to identify with the mother and father figures and other adults in the works. He explains that in the life-and-death conditions of World War Two:

> Le père de famille se trouve alors confronté à un cas de conscience: il ne veut, il ne peut en aucune façon mettre la vie des siens en péril. Une maman, nous le savons tous, ne veut en aucun cas se trouver séparée de ses enfants. (**243**)

His works therefore have a moral perspective, opening up questions of identity for all ages of readership. This perspective, with its strong sense of message, has a double quality. It comes as from an outsider—an adult reflecting on the events of his youth— and yet he is the insider, especially in his most strictly autobiographical works of which *Un sac de billes* and *Baby-foot* are the most widely read examples. He stands both outside the events of his life, setting them into a framework of ideas and moralities, and also inside them as he recounts the events as they happen.

Being both an insider and an outsider is a theme taken up by Fred Kupferman, in his «Postface» to the 1982 Livre de Poche 'Jeunesse', in relation to Jewish identity. He writes: '… à l'âge où un écolier apprend ses leçons, un enfant juif apprend à survivre' (p. 379). The notion of Jewish identity is of particular interest in the French context. In 1791, the French National Assembly gave Jews full French citizenship. This meant that they were no longer part of a juridically recognised, distinct community. They had rights and duties under a Republican state equal to all other French citizens. The principles of 'Liberté, Égalité, Fraternité' applied to them all.

Yet this decision by the National Assembly was problematic for Jews. On the one hand it could not be disputed that they had an identity. This was based on religious beliefs within a secular state, a strong sense of shared Jewish heritage and past, and a separate language. As Joffo explains in his 'Dialogue avec mes lecteurs':

> Je vous dirai maintenant ce que signifie pour moi être juif, en France ou ailleurs, au vingtième siècle. Je pense que c'est être héritier d'une grande tradition religieuse qui remonte à Abraham, père des grandes religions monothéistes, à Moïse, le prophète des prophètes, le seul homme qui ait rencontré Dieu, qui l'ait entendu. (247)

On the other hand, the decision meant that juridically they were not different. Their identity was that of Frenchness. In theory a separate Jewish identity could not exist alongside the French identity and could lead to assimilation of the Jews within the French state. In many ways this is a similar problem to that faced since the 1970s by Muslim French people in France.

The Dreyfus Affair (1894-1906), in particular, opened up the issue, masked by the decision of the National Assembly, of separate identity versus that of assimilation in the context of growing anti-semitism in the twentieth century. Given this assimilation, of no separate identity being given under the state to Jewishness, Jean-Paul Sartre in his *Réflexions sur la question juive* states that a specific Jewish identity is created by the anti-Semite who projects onto the Jew sets of negative identities. He gives examples of how the anti-semite falsely ascribes distinguishing negative, physical, moral and other attributes of identity to the Jews in France, creating difference where there is none, in an attempt to justify his anti-Semitism: 'Loin que l'expérience engendre la notion de Juif, c'est celle-ci qui éclaire l'expérience au contraire; si le Juif n'existait pas, l'antisémite l'inventerait' (*13*, pp. 14-15).

The Jew is therefore forced to see himself not only through his own eyes, but also through the eyes of the anti-Semite. As shown, particularly in *Un sac de billes*, this leads to a complex set of identities for the Jew. The first is related to notions of 'Liberté, Égalité, Fraternité', of being the same as other French people. The second is a double identity, being on the one hand a heightened awareness of the negative aspects of Jewish identity as perceived by those subscribing to anti-Semitism, and on the other hand, as a reaction, a heightened, positive awareness of belonging to the Jewish heritage and culture. The negative connotations of Jewishness are given by Joffo, quoting Hitler's *Mein Kampf*:

> Le juif est et demeure le parasite-type, l'écornifleur, qui tel un bacille nuisible s'étend toujours plus loin, sitôt qu'un sol nourricier favorable l'y invite. L'effet produit par sa présence est celui des plantes parasites! Là où il se fixe, le peuple qui l'accueille s'éteint au bout d'un temps plus ou moins long. (**246**)

The Jew is therefore both a self and an Other and it is this aspect that gives Joffo's works their special qualities. He demonstrates the awareness of a developing 'normal, French' self through the thoughts and actions of a child, while at the same time he evokes the development of the Jewish child's awareness of himself as an Other. Joffo's own comments from his standpoint of an adult in *Un sac de billes* and *Baby-foot* put these internal developments into a wider historical, evaluative context.

Focusing on the development of the child and the child's awareness of his or her personal and cultural identity, it is natural that Joffo should use the notion of play and games as a central structuring device. The two titles *Un sac de billes* and *Baby-foot* clearly stress the notion of play. Play enables children to test out and develop skills and reactions that relate to real-life situations but which are safe within the context of the game. However, by juxtaposing play and real-life situations within his works, Joffo is able to make full use of the symbolism of play. The need to capture an opponent's marbles can turn into the reality of capture by the

Germans at the whim of fortune, and thus serve his purpose of enabling the reader to explore childhood identity and Jewish identity at one and the same time from a position of security.

Equally, this sense of enabling the young reader in particular to experience traumatic events with security is fostered by the fictional frameworks that Joffo employs, for example storytelling and fairy-tale imagery. Storytelling assumes coherence even when the events are chaotic. Fairy tales articulate life and death experiences, again within a coherent structure based on familiar, repeated devices and images. They are safe, as coherent fictions, but, as with play, the real-life situations which they imitate are juxtaposed. The apparent illusion of the fictional framework can mask the reality that suddenly emerges. The grandmother on the train to Dax, who asks Jo and Maurice questions, looks just like the illustrations in the books Jo has read, but her questions make him realise he cannot trust anyone any more. The lemonade she offers is at the centre of a subsequent nightmare by Jo involving the SS (**38-41**).

This relationship between fiction and real life is an important feature of the genre of autobiography. On the simplest level, autobiography is usually different from pure fiction in that, however life-threatening the events of the autobiography, the reader is able to experience them in security. The reader knows that Jo must survive since his adult self is writing at a future date about the events, and commenting on them as he writes. It is not fiction, but neither is it a documentation of an historical moment. As Laura Marcus writes:

> For the most part, however, the value of autobiography is seen to lie in its 'insider' quality: the autonomous status of autobiography is based on its separation from forms of history-writing, where history was and is defined as an 'objective', 'documentary' approach to lives and events. (*14*, p. 5)

Autobiography is not merely a recounting of the events of the writer's life. It is a construct:

> ... in selecting, ordering, and integrating the writer's lived experiences according to its own teleological demands, the autobiographical narrative is beholden to certain imperatives of imaginative discourse. Autobiography, in short, transforms empirical facts into *artifacts. (15,* p. 269)

The work of art that is created is articulated according to a cultural perspective:

> All knowing and all telling are subject to the conventions of art. Because we apprehend reality through culturally determined types, we can report the most particular event only in the form of a representational fiction, assigning motives, causes, and effects according to our best lights rather than according to absolute truth. (*16*, p. 151)

Equally there are variations in the levels of subjectivity within the genre of autobiography. Leo Bersani evaluates two different approaches to writing about the historical moment. He compares Malraux's *La Condition humaine* with Bataille's *Le Bleu du ciel.* The first, set in 1927, is based on the split between Chiang Kai-shek and the Communists, a significant moment in the development of Chinese politics. The second, set in 1934, is based on the place of a workers' insurrection in the context of the rise of Nazism. Bersani states that *La Condition humaine*: 'is about people whose most intimate consciousness of themselves seems to be almost indistinguishable from their political passions, and *Le Bleu du ciel* can be seen as 'a wholly personal account of [...] a year that coincidentally is one of great fascist and communist unrest in Europe' (*17*, p. 102).

*Un sac de billes* and *Baby-foot* reflect this difference. The former is set in a period during which the questions of Jo's personal identity as someone who happens to be a Jew and his other negative identity as a Jew are inextricable. Jo stands not only for himself but also for the Jewish nation. The Occupation of France by the Germans and the institution of the Vichy regime is more than a historical setting for his adventures with Maurice. It is a defining moment in history for a nation and for Jews, with France no longer a Republic based on the notions of 'Liberté, Égalité, Fraternité' but a French State based on 'Travail, Famille, Patrie' from which the Jews were excluded. In the case of *Baby-foot*, however, the historical moment does not serve the same purpose. France was once again a Republic, and Jews were no longer under the same threat. While undeniably a period of significant political and cultural change after the Liberation, the context serves rather as the background against which Jo is defining himself. The work is more akin to a *Bildungsroman* or *roman d'éducation* in the way in which it shows Jo learning personal lessons and reflecting upon them, developing thus a personal identity that is separate from his Jewish one.

These, then, are not works of exact historical documentation, and yet there is much to be learnt about the detail of the period. Nor are they works of fiction, and yet there is much that has been constructed in a fictional manner. Joffo's purposes are multiple. The works serve his own purpose, enabling him to write about his life as a form of exorcism, but he has a clear warning message for his readers, be they children or adults:

> Si aujourd'hui la France devait à nouveau traverser une grave crise économique, avec cinq ou six millions de chômeurs, cela ferait, je crois, le jeu de ceux qui prêchent la xénophobie, le racisme, et bien sûr l'antisémitisme. (**246**)

# Contexts

## The historical and political context

As stated in the previous chapter, there are clear differences between the role and prominence of the historical and political contexts of the two novels. *Un sac de billes* is firmly set in the context of France in World War Two after its defeat by the Germans in 1940. The novel starts in 1941 (**10-11**) in the rue de Clignancourt at the heart of the Jewish sector (**145**) in the XVIII<sup>e</sup> *arrondissement* of Paris, an area which had seen the arrival of many of the estimated forty thousand refugees from the anti-Jewish pogroms in Russia and Eastern Europe at the end of the nineteenth century and first half of the twentieth century (**9**). It ends in Paris with the Liberation of France in 1944. The many references to political and social events in World War Two France form a dense underpinning to the adventures of Jo and Maurice and cannot be separated from the plot of *Un sac de billes*. *Baby-foot* starts in post-Liberation France but, while there are still references to the French-based context of political and social change during the period, they function primarily as a background setting for the events rather than as a principal focus. Instead it is the references to the increasing American cultural influence that become dominant, as the focus shifts to Jo's personal development, his ideals and his aspirations.

### The war years: defeat and Occupation

The Occupied and Unoccupied Zones that came into being in 1940 were divided by a demarcation line. The only way of crossing it legally was by a pass issued by the Germans. Since many of the thousands of French people wishing to cross were Jews who could not obtain a pass, they had, like Jo and Maurice (**57-58**), to cross it illegally with the help of a *passeur*. However, the difference between the two zones was not as great as they might have imagined. The 'France libre' of which Jo dreams while at Dax (**47**) was little different from the Occupied Zone they were fleeing. This is symbolised by Jo's reaction once he and Maurice are on the other side of the line, since he cannot see any difference from before the line (**58**). Indeed, in reality it soon became apparent that the Vichy government in the Unoccupied Zone would do little that was against the wishes of the Germans. It became very clear that there were many in the government—and in the whole of France—who supported the Germans, seeing them as a means of bringing stability and strength to the country after the weaknesses of the Third Republic.

> If the Occupation was a period of savage constraint, there were many French people—by no means confined to the Right—who also saw it as an opportunity to set about tasks that had been beyond the powers of the Third Republic [...]. This was the opportunity to rebuild society and government on the old certainties and disciplines of the traditional moral order, the neglect of which had allegedly contributed to the military defeat of 1940. (*1*, p. 89)

This attitude is shown clearly in *Un sac de billes* in the characters of Ambroise Mancelier and his son Raoul. Raoul states that France ought to have joined with Hitler and Mussolini from 1936 to take over England and Russia (**207**). Mancelier echoes this vision of a Europe controlled by strength, and says that the reason France did not follow such a path was the fault of the Jews in the government at the time (**208**), i.e. the Front populaire government of Léon Blum. The Jews, according to Mancelier, were linked to other groups who helped to weaken France, i.e. foreigners, freemasons and socialists (**208**). Three heroes are quoted by Mancelier: Louis XIV, Napoléon and Pétain, because of their vision of the strength of France within Europe, as an ally of Germany (**206-7**).

Politically, the Manceliers are supporters of Pétain and, in particular, Pierre Laval, the man who became head of government in April 1942. While Pétain could be credited with having an heroic past as a result of his action at Verdun in World War One, and in sensing that an armistice was the only way of preserving France as a country, Laval was much more sympathetic to the Germans and their aims.

The old count whom Jo and Maurice meet on their journey is equally anti-republican, but he contrasts with the Manceliers in being adamantly anti-German. He represents traditional French monarchist ideals, regretting the introduction of the republic and the disappearance of the monarchy, since, according to the count, only the monarchy could have stood up to the Germans and retained the independence of France, and its traditional pre-republican values of greatness, sacrifice, order and purity (**71-72**).

Pétain did not wait long before abolishing the French Republic and instituting 'L'Etat Français'. His 'Loi constitutionnelle' of 10 July 1940 replaced 'Liberté, Égalité, Fraternité' by 'Travail, Famille, Patrie'. The main article of the new constitution specified that:

> L'Assemblée nationale donne tout pouvoir au gouvernement de la République, sous l'autorité et la signature du maréchal PÉTAIN, à l'effet de promulguer par un ou plusieurs actes une nouvelle Constitution de l'État français. Cette Constitution devra garantir les droits du travail, de la famille et de la patrie.

The contrasting principles underpinning these two mottos structure *Un sac de billes*. They are introduced early in the work when Jo's father is telling the story of how their family's ancestors fled the massacres in Eastern Europe, travelled west and crossed a frontier. The first thing they saw was a large building with the republican motto «Liberté—Égalité—Fraternité» on it. They knew that they were in France and that the republican motto would guarantee their safety (**19**). Jo links the motto with a debate about national pride and the love his father has for his country of adoption. Jo's father is still convinced at this point in the novel that they will be safe as Jews, but Jo's mother has doubts.

Ironically the new motto, if taken literally, shows Jo and his family to be the very model of the new French citizens to which the

French State aspired. They work hard, they are a very close-knit family and they love their country. But, as Jews, they were not in control of the principles underpinning the new motto. As Jews they had no rights to live or work in the new state. They were to be excluded from the very country they loved. The episode with Mancelier towards the end of *Un sac de billes* explores this issue of the right to belong to a family, community or country. Mancelier tells Jo that, by living and working in his house, he is a member of the Mancelier family. But belonging brings commitments, and in this case the proof of commitment is to go to Mass with the Mancelier family. Only then will Jo be a true member of the family. As a Jew, however, he knows he cannot take part in Mass, and knows that he cannot be a member of the family on Mancelier's terms. In the event he does go to Mass, but for his own personal reasons, the main one of which is to be able to be close to Françoise, Mancelier's young daughter (**203**).

## The Jews in World War Two

The opening chapters of *Un sac de billes* quickly set the scene based on the historical facts of 1941 and 1942. There is some ambiguity concerning the year the novel begins depending on the edition. The original Lattès edition sets the opening of the work in 1942, while the *Livre de Poche* edition changes this to 1941. As stated in the opening chapter, however, *Un sac de billes* is much more than a work of historical documentation. Events are used to give a general context against which to set the plot. Thus, if the setting is 1941, it is a historical fact that the SS would be in the streets of Paris (**12**) as they had been since the fall of France, and the barber's shop would have a sign outside marking it out in German and French as Jewish (**13**) as had been required since October 1940. It is not chronologically correct that Jo would have to wear a yellow star with the word 'Juif' on it (**20**): the law obliging all Jews aged six and above to wear a yellow star was introduced only in May 1942.

Whether documented with chronological accuracy or not, the major details of the oppression of the Jews are given, particularly in *Un sac de billes*. Along with the restrictions noted above, the whole question of Jewish identity within the new French State is explored. In September 1940 there was a census of Jews carried out by the 'Préfectures' in the Occupied Zone under the orders of the Germans. A similar census was carried out in the Unoccupied Zone by the Vichy government in June 1941. It was possible therefore to know how many Jews there were and where they lived. This was followed in October 1940 by legislation specifying Jewish identity and forcing Jews to have their identity cards marked with the word 'Juif' or 'Juive' (**20**). Jews were identified as such if their grandparents had been Jewish, and Jews were forbidden to work for the state, the press or cinema. Once identifiable, it became possible for the French State to begin the process of arresting them, with the aim of sending them to extermination camps. In March 1941 the Commissariat général aux questions juives (CGQJ) was set up to introduce legislation concerning Jews and to oversee its application. In June 1941 Jews were excluded from most of the occupations not already covered by law, and no more than 3% of Jewish children were permitted to attend Secondary schools. The following month the authorities in the Occupied Zone introduced a law seizing all Jewish possessions and businesses—the so-called 'economic arianisation'—and forbidding Jews to go out between 8 pm and 6 am, to appear in public, or to own a radio, bicycle or phone (**21**). Anti-Jewish posters of the sort seen by Jo (**23-24**) were rife.

In May, August and December 1941, thousands of Jews were rounded up in Paris and sent to Drancy, a concentration camp near Paris. July 1942 saw the most notorious event, the arrest by some four and a half thousand French police of approximately 13,000 Jews and their rounding-up at the *Vel'd'Hiv* (Vélodrome d'hiver) before being sent to Drancy, Beaune-la-Rolande ou Pithiviers, and then on to Auschwitz. This is probably the incident to which Henri refers (**98**). Fortunately their parents had left just before the arrests, but they still ended up in the camp at Pau, imprisoned by the Vichy authorities. In August 1942, there was a series of arrests in the

Unoccupied Zone followed by more in Marseilles in January 1943. By the end of the war, out of a total of 300,000 Jews in France, more than 75,000 had been deported to German extermination camps. Out of these, less than 3,000 survived.

It is the danger of being a Jew in Paris in 1941 that forces Jo's family to send the two boys away to safety in the Unoccupied Zone. This was, of course, a false safety. Despite their father's attempts to make them never admit that they are Jewish (**33-34**), they are at risk everywhere in the Occupied Zone and, from November 1942 when the Germans took over the Unoccupied Zone, they are at risk there as well. Much of *Un sac de billes* concerns the Gestapo and their search for Jews in Nice, their headquarters being the Hôtel Excelsior. Jo and Maurice cannot admit to being Jewish, knowing that such an admission would seal their fate. They are interrogated and, like many Jews at the time, are given a physical examination by the doctor. It is clear that they have both been circumcised. Circumcision has been for some 3,500 years the sign of Jewish identity, based on the instruction issued by God to Abraham in *Genesis*, XVII, 10-14. The doctor, however, tells the German officer that their circumcision is a surgical operation (**162**). It is a close escape. Jo recounts a few pages later how the Germans came to the Compagnons de France camp, inspected the children and took away those who were circumcised. Among them is Masso, whose circumcision is, indeed, surgical. He is denied the opportunity to explain this to them, the Germans needing to make up the numbers for the convoy. He is taken away and Jo never sees him again, but he knows what his fate was (**168-9**).

## Resistance, collaboration and liberation

### a) Resistance

Resistance and collaboration are major themes of *Un sac de billes*. The notion of resistance was at the heart of the famous 18 June 1940 speech broadcast by de Gaulle from London, in which he called upon the French to stand up for their country and to resist. It is ironic that the Vichy government stripped de Gaulle of his French nationality in December 1940. He became as non-French as Jo and the Jewish inhabitants of France were to become.

While there have been debates about the extent of the French Resistance movement and its effectiveness, there is no doubt about its strength in certain parts of France, and its role in helping the French regain their sense of pride after the defeat of 1940. There were two main choices open to the French who wanted to resist—to join de Gaulle and his FFL (Forces françaises libres), a military resistance outside France, or to become engaged in resistance inside France, to be called from 1944 FFI (Forces françaises de l'intérieur) (218), either as a member of a group creating escape networks and publishing clandestine newspapers, or as an individual performing acts of humanitarian benefit. It is the various forms of resistance within France that Jo encounters.

The Resistance movement in the Unoccupied Zone was initially different from that in the Occupied Zone, since the perceived enemy was different. In the Occupied Zone it was the Germans, and any form of organised opposition ran very serious risks. In the Unoccupied Zone, the main enemy was Vichy France and its government. Until the Germans took over the Unoccupied Zone in November 1942, much of the resistance was based on propaganda, for example *Combat*, a paper produced from the end of 1941 by the Combat group headed by Henri Frenay. It was only from 1942 that some form of co-ordination took place, set up by Jean Moulin in liaison with de Gaulle. It was he who succeeded in bringing together the main groups in the south of France in 1943 to create the MUR (Mouvements Unis de la Résistance).

Until 1943, the numbers of people actively engaged in resistance were small. They were mainly those who were committed to resistance for ideological or intellectual reasons. Paradoxically it was the Germans who caused the spread of resistance to embrace ordinary people, by introducing in February 1943 the STO (Service du Travail Obligatoire). The Germans had the right to force any Frenchman to go to work in Germany to replace German workers who were now needed in the German army. Jo's brothers Henri and Albert are called up for service in the STO (**112-4**) while they are living in Menton, and they decide to escape for Nice that very night in order to avoid forced labour. For the first time in the war, many average Frenchmen were affected directly, and the result was 'desertion' to the countryside, and the setting up of the *maquis*, groups of resistance members living and acting in secret in the countryside. Organisations like the MUR trained and fed them, but the *maquis* groups acted largely on their own initiative, deciding for themselves the nature of their guerrilla warfare, rather than being organised and controlled from outside. The number of people in the *maquis* has been estimated at between thirty and fifty thousand, and most of the groups were in the south, especially in the inaccessible mountainous areas.

Jo and Maurice experience the different aspects of the Resistance movement at first hand. Their arrest in Nice is a result of Ferdinand visiting a house he thinks is that of a Resistance group supplying false papers, as many did. It is of course a trap (**151**). Later, Jo and Maurice want to join the 'maquis', but it appears they are still too young (**208**). Maurice is proud to be working for a cook who is a member of the Resistance movement and who listens to the BBC (**208**), something which had been outlawed by the German authorities. Consequently listening to it was not only a means of gathering information, but also, in itself, an act of resistance. At the end of *Un sac de billes*, Jo does succeed in becoming a helper of the Resistance movement when he delivers a message to a «M. Jean» (**212-4**). As he explains, however, it was his only contribution to the fight for a free France.

Other forms of resistance are encountered. One significant figure in *Un sac de billes*—as in reality—is the Bishop of Nice, Mgr Rémond. He was not typical of the Catholic Church which has been much criticised for its non-critical attitude towards Hitler. Historically the Catholic Church had been anti-Jewish, seeing the Jews as responsible for the death of Christ. Within France it was criticised for putting its own political and institutional interests above those of the French people, refusing to protest against the atrocities committed against the French Jews. In particular, the 1905 Act separating the power of the state from that of the Church, and the anti-Church stance of many Republican leaders, made the Catholic Church sympathise with right-wing movements that they hoped would return France to the pre-1905 situation. Consequently many within the Church were not opposed to Pétain and the ending of the Republic, and gave their tacit support to Vichy and the Germans.

It has also been argued, however, that the Church was not fully aware, especially at the beginning of the war, of the extent and nature of the atrocities committed against the Jews, and there is evidence of protests by the Church and an increasing attitude of support for resistance. For example, after the *Vel'd'hiv* episode, the Assembly of Cardinals and Archbishops in the Occupied Zone did protest to the government. There were even more protests in the Unoccupied Zone by senior members of the Church, in particular Mgr Saliège (mentioned by Joffo in the 'Dialogue avec mes lecteurs' [239]) in Toulouse; Mgr Théas (Montauban); Mgr Delay (Marseille); Mgr Moussaron (Albi); Mgr Vanstenberghe (Bayonne); Cardinal Gerlier (Lyon). The protests of Mgr Théas and Cardinal Gerlier were broadcast by the BBC from London in September 1942.

Mgr Rémond, Bishop of Nice, was one of those in the Catholic Church who tried to help the persecuted. He saved more than five hundred Jewish children by arranging false papers establishing their Catholic identity. Subinagui mentions him as the source of false baptismal cerificates, and Joffo notes that he thus saved many children from going to Drancy (**177**).

There were equally many priests who helped in the fight against the occupying forces. It is a priest who, by his stubborn politeness, enables Jo and Maurice to 'prove' their Catholic identity at the Hôtel Excelsior and so be released. Joffo comments on the ambiguous position of the Gestapo in relation to the Catholic Church, stating that: 'la politique de collaboration européenne n'est pas encore abandonnée, il ne faut donc pas, sous prétexte d'envoyer deux gosses dans la chambre à gaz, se brouiller avec l'Église française car les pratiquants sont nombreux' (**181**). It is another priest who helps Jo and Maurice to leave the train at Dax by telling the SS that they are with him (**44-45**). This is a lie, but the priest says that he treats all children as part of his responsibility, and so, in effect, they were with him.

Another example of resistance is that of Subinagui at the Compagnons de France. The movement was founded in 1940 in the Unoccupied Zone by Henry Dhavernas. He was concerned that the war had created many thousands of refugee children who had been cut off from their families, and he wanted to give them support and help. His ideas ironically coincided with those of the Vichy government to train French youth to serve the new French State. Marshal Pétain himself came to the first meeting of the Compagnons de France in the forest of Randan in August 1940 to give the movement his seal of approval. The Compagnons were organised as 'Compagnies', each of which contained five teams of ten boys aged from fourteen to nineteen. They were given a uniform (**134**) and, like Jo and Maurice, work to do in the local community. By the end of 1940 there were more than ten thousand teenagers in the movement, of whom 70% were refugees. Early in 1941, Dhavernas left the movement amid growing apprehension by the Vichy government that it was proving to be too independent, and could not be controlled by the government. In May 1941, Guillaume de Tournemire, an independent-minded cavalry officer was elected as leader by the movement, against the wishes of the government. The movement then began to become increasingly critical of Vichy. It sheltered not only refugees from the north, but also those who had escaped from the STO. It provided false papers or arranged for boys to hide and work with the 'maquis', and one of its periodicals criticised the *Vel' d'hiv* arrests in July 1942. It continued to help refugee children, in particular Jewish ones. De Tournemire himself, along with many of the other members of the organisation, was an active members of the Resistance movement and, once the south of France was occupied by the Germans, de Tournemire's position became very difficult. He managed to escape arrest in 1942, but in 1943 he went into hiding himself. The movement was dissolved by the government in 1944. Subinagui, by

his involvement in the Resistance movement and his help in giving
Jo, Maurice and the other children a safe home and then by helping
them to escape (186), is totally in the spirit of the leaders of the
movement.

In *Baby-foot*, the allusions to resistance are rare and only indirect.
Jo does organise a secret network, but it is for the purpose of selling
surplus stocks of chewing gum on the black market, and is referred
to as a spy network (39). The police are feared by Jo, but not
because they might arrest him for being a Jew, rather because he is
delivering black market goods (47).


## b) Collaboration


In the atmosphere of World War Two France, in which
resistance was clandestine, it was not always possible to distinguish
between those who supported the Resistance movement and those
who collaborated with the occupying forces. When Henri goes to
the transit camp in Pau to try to save his parents, he succeeds when
Colonel T. telephones Paris and appears to receive the information
that his parents are not Jewish. The brothers speculate on how that
can have happened, since they are Jewish. While there might have
been careless administration, Albert suggests that there might be
someone in the 'Préfecture' who wants to help those in difficulty. Jo
himself proposes an ingenious solution, that Colonel T. might have
invented the replies he received over the telephone (110-1),
appearing therefore to collaborate with the Germans, but in fact
working against them. However, as becomes clear, Jo later changes
his mind, since Albert and Henri shortly afterwards receive orders
to leave for the STO (113). Less ambiguous in the event, though not
at the time, is Doctor Rosen. He, a Jew, appears to be helping the
Germans at the Hôtel Excelsior, but he tells the SS that the boys'
circumcision is not a result of their Jewish identity, but is the result
of an operation. In the 'Dialogue avec mes lecteurs', Joffo lists him
among those who worked to save France (238).

In fact it became almost impossible to distinguish collaborators from resistance workers on the basis what they appeared to be doing or saying. Jo and Maurice, like the rest of the population, lived in a country in which nobody could trust anyone else. They are taught by their father from the outset never to admit, even to a friend, that they are Jewish (33-34). At «Moisson Nouvelle» they do not talk to those who came from families supporting Pétain since it is impossible even to trust a friend (144). Those who appear friendly may easily be collaborators, as Jo and Maurice discover when the chef at the Hôtel Excelsior sets a trap for them, hoping that they will attempt to escape while picking tomatoes and be shot by a hidden soldier (178-9). At the beginning of the novel, Jo's teacher M. Boulier treats Jo as a non-person now that he wears the star showing that he is Jewish (24-25). Later, at Marseilles station, they learn that the gendarmes—figures normally of authority and trust—have orders to arrest any Jews (74). Conversely, those who fit the stereotype of the collaborator, can easily turn out not to be so, for example Madame Vouillard who questions Jo and Maurice, and whom Jo suspects is someone who will denounce them. It quickly transpires that she is Jewish and is quite innocent (196-8).

As with the rare allusions to resistance, *Baby-foot* contains few allusions to collaboration. Those that are made are indirect, the most significant one being the punishment meted out by Jo on Fouloche. Fouloche is not of course a collaborator, but the organiser of a protection racket. However, the incident is given the vocabulary and connotations relevant to collaboration. Jo is worried that someone in his own group of friends—a traitor to his cause (76)—may have informed Fouloche of the ambush and Jo's friends hide, rather like the *maquis* behind trees ('fusains', 74). Jo does not 'denounce' Fouloche in front of the class (68), and he punishes him by shaving his hair. This was a widespread punishment particularly of women in the years immediately following the Liberation. Sartre, in his column in *Combat* on 2 September 1944, writes that it recalls the sadism of the Middle Ages. The widespread nature of the punishment, and the fact that it was often carried out publicly gave the French people a sense of purifying their country after the

Occupation, and to a certain extent, of returning to their old values. Jo adopts the punishment technique, but modifies it to leave a small tuft of hair at the front like an Iroquois Indian, a sign that while his past experiences still influence him, the focus is elsewhere, in particular the influence of America that came with the Liberation.

### c) Liberation

The Liberation of France and the immediate postwar period are the setting for *Baby-foot*, as is clearly indicated in the first pages of the novel. On 6 June 1944, the allied forces landed in Normandy, and by August that year, de Gaulle was in Paris heading a provisional government. The end of the war was officially May 1945, the year in which *Baby-foot* begins (9). Jo also mentions *Franc-Tireur* (10), the newspaper of one of the main Resistance movements in the south of Occupied France, produced in secret during the war, and which produced its first free version on 21 August 1944. The death of his father in a concentration camp is one of the first facts mentioned (11) by Jo, along with the sight of his mother (42) and other Jews (23-24) who have returned and who are aged before their time as a result of their experience.

*Baby-foot* focuses less, however, on the experience of historical and political events, than on Jo's personal experience, and the way he is developing as an individual. Historical terminology is still there, but, as in the case of the incident with Fouloche, the interpretation is different, the signifier shifting from a historical or political signified to a different cultural or other signified. For example, Jo mentions 'le jour J' (D-Day), but it refers not to 6 June 1944, the beginning of the liberation of France, rather to the day he will make his delivery of black market goods (49). Similarly, Jo has a dream of a statue with the word 'LIBERTÉ' underneath it, but this no longer has the full connotations of the republican motto that abound in *Un sac de billes*. 'Liberté' has become a symbol of his personal freedom as he dreams of going to the south of France again (169). Equally, de Gaulle is mentioned (54), but it is significant that he is not seen by Jo as a leader of great significance for the French nation, nor even as one of his own heroes, merely as someone on one of the extremes of politics opposite Thorez, the Communist leader, who is mentioned in the same sentence. Jo's real heroes are Napoléon Bonaparte, Julius Caesar and Eisenhower, the last being the supreme commander of the Allied Expeditionary Force, who led the assault on the Germans beginning in Normandy (80). It is the influence of America and American culture and symbols that is one of the main features of *Baby-foot*, part of a social and cultural context that shapes Jo far more than the political and historical events within France.

## The social and cultural context

### Rationing and the black market

Both novels contain much material about the hardships endured during the Occupation and afterwards, in particular rationing and the resulting black market. As early as 1 September 1939, the government brought in a law enabling the distribution of food to be controlled when the need arose. This law was first put into effect in November 1939, forbidding the sale of fresh meat on three days of the week. By 5 March 1940, the *Journal Officiel* introduced the idea of rationing certain products according to age and need, and, by 23 September 1940, food rationing was introduced across France. It was not that there was not enough food in France for the French; rather it was the Germans who needed the supplies. A typical four-person family in 1940 had the right to about 9.8 kilos of bread, 1.44 kilos of meat, 0.2 kilos of cheese, 0.4 kilos of fat (butter and oil) and 0.5 kilos of sugar a week—if they could find a supplier. Jo and Maurice encounter the shortage of food at Dax. There is no milk at the station café, and ration tickets—of which they have none—are needed for bread (**45**). The meal at Hagetmau is equally frugal, and the bill 'salée', i.e. exaggeratedly high (**50**). The ration decreased steadily throughout the war. The number of calories this represented went down from about 1,200 a day to well below 1,000 by the end of the war. Jo describes how, at the end of 1943, he altered ration tickets with the figure 4 on them—those allowing purchase of starchy foods such as potatoes—to ones with a 1 on them—those allowing the purchase of sugar, a much more precious and rare commodity during the war (**199-200**).

The Vichy government, with the family at the centre of its new motto, did try to ensure a distribution of vitamin-enhanced biscuits to all children from six to fourteen, as Jo recounts (**102**). These usually came with the instruction that they were not to be given to Jews or foreigners, though in most schools they were distributed nevertheless.

Along with food, petrol was very strictly limited, and driving was forbidden unless a special permit was obtained. Consequently there was a boom in other forms of transport. The comte de V. explains how his car has been requisitioned by the Germans, and so he has to travel by horse and carriage (**70-71**). Trains were overcrowded, as Jo describes for the journey to Dax (**36-37**), and increasingly rare as the war continued, in particular because of the disruption caused by attacks on the lines by the *maquis* (**188**). Bicycles became highly-prized possessions, rising in price almost fourfold on the black market by 1942. Jo recounts the difficulties not only of obtaining a bicycle, but the tyres as well. The only way was by barter, a second-hand tyre being worth 'les yeux de la tête, c'est-à-dire cinq cartouches de cigarettes, dix pour la paire' (**117**).

Clothing, too, was rationed from 1941, bringing in its wake the need to repair worn-out clothing and ingenuity in planning for harsh weather. Jo and Maurice want to buy clothes at a shop in Montluçon, but the shop-keeper can only offer scarves made of *ersatz* artificial fibre (**192**). When Jo and Maurice are in Menton they need material for their school wear since without it they cannot go to school. Fortunately Albert has managed to accumulate enough textile coupons for them, and they are able to have it made (**100-1**). Shoes, too, after January 1941, could only be bought with ration tokens, following a ban introduced in December 1940 on shoes with thick leather soles. The result was the introduction of wooden-soled shoes, to which Jo makes an allusion in *Baby-foot* (195).

The black market started as early as December 1940. The government did not condemn the black market, as long as any transaction was to supply personal or family needs, but, as early as 1941, Maréchal Pétain denounced its immorality when profit was involved. In fact it became a necessity for most French people in order to supplement their rations and consequently was very widespread, being organised not only on an individual basis by those who had access to items they could sell, but also in organised networks. In *Un sac de billes*, Jo describes the complex workings of his own black market business. He realises that the Italians were willing to exchange their surplus supplies of oil for vegetables and, starting from that premise, exchanges the tomatoes he is able to obtain for their oil, which he then sells. With the money and the stolen cigarettes given to him, he buys rice on the black market, which he then exchanges for flour which he then sells. With the profit he is able to buy more tomatoes and start all over again (**116**). The principle was no different for large-scale business, except that this is too rich for Jo's blood, being based on a three-way exchange of wine, petrol and cigarettes (123).

The scarcity of products meant that black market prices rose. As an indication of the difference between official prices and those of the black market in June 1944, the official prices for the following articles were: 1 litre of milk cost 4.6 francs (the black market price was four to six times as much); a dozen eggs cost 36 francs (the black market price was three times as much); 1 kilo of butter cost 78 francs (the black market price was six to eight times as much) and cooking oil at 50 francs a litre was sold on the black market for twenty times as much, nearly as much as the monthly wage of a worker at the time: 1,100 francs. The result, as with the clothing, was an increase in artificial products, for example the barley-based coffee and saccharine sweetener at Dax (**45**).

The end of the war did not see an immediate end to the suffering caused by the lack of goods and food. Ration quotas were deliberately increased by the government, but it was merely a

Jo notes early in *Baby-foot* that: 'Avec les troupes
américaines, la liberté est entrée, mais le charbon n'a pas suivi' (17).

The Americans may not have brought coal, but they did bring
many of the goods that fed the black market. During World War
Two, one billion sets of rations were produced by the Americans
for their combat troops. Rations included biscuits, cereals, coated
peanuts or raisins, soluble coffee, sugar, lemon- or orange-juice
powder, jam, hot chocolate powder, cigarettes, chewing gum and
canned meats. In addition, American tobacco companies sent
millions of free cigarettes to the soldiers in Europe. In theory all
these rations and goods were intended for front-line forces, but in
practice, many found their way onto the black market. In *Baby-foot*,
Greenbaum works under a colonel in charge of dealing with
surpluses in the provision of cigarettes and sweets to American
soldiers (35). Greenbaum hints at the excess of such supplies when
he offers Jo chewing gum. The gap between Jo's ideal and the offer
from Greenbaum is eloquent:

> Je pense: «Dix à quinze paquets ce serait formidable!»
> Greenbaum sifflote, s'arrête, regarde les étoiles froides entre les
> nuages.
> «Trois camions, dit-il. O.K.?» (33)

The result was the continuation of the black market to
supplement everyday life, whether it be luxuries such as chewing
gum and American cigarettes or everyday goods such as flour,
which was still seen as a commodity worth trading on the black
market (56-57). The end of the novel describes the black market
operation of the American soldier Sterling Boydt. He is delivering
nylons to the south of France in boxes marked 'Explosives' (174),
and later returns to Paris laden with boxes of shoes (195).

## The influence of America

As outlined above, it is the new influence of American culture and society that has the greatest influence on Jo. André Malraux, a future Minister of Culture under de Gaulle, was clearly aware of the new role America was to play when he said in an interview in 1945:

> Il y a quelque chose de profond qui rassemble subtilement l'Amérique, l'Angleterre, la France, le Portugal et l'Espagne. C'est le futur d'une nouvelle culture. Après la guerre de 1914-1918, l'humanité crut que l'événement le plus transcendantal avait été la bataille de Verdun. Et pourtant, ce fut la révolution russe de 1917. De même, il n'y aurait rien d'étonnant que, lorsqu'on fera l'histoire de cette guerre, on découvre que l'événement le plus influent sur la destinée du monde ne soit pas la bataille de Stalingrad, ni le débarquement de Normandie, ni l'effondrement militaire du nazisme, mais la conférence de Rio de Janeiro, premier symptôme de l'unité américaine. (*18*, p. 29)

The American way of life represented by the GIs on the streets, films, music and sports was an ideal that could be a dream for the French in general and for Jo in particular as he aspires to a new future. References to American chewing gum abound in *Baby-foot* and form the centre-piece of a description of its rarity—and therefore its value—in postwar France. Jo claims that his first piece lasted two weeks and describes his horror at swallowing it by accident after a playground fight (36). Cigarettes are no longer merely cigarettes, or even the 'cigarettes pour asthmatiques' (14) that he used to buy. They are now referred to by their brand names reflecting their American origin, such as *Camel* or *Lucky Strike*, the two leading American brands:

> Je prends une Camel de la main gauche et plonge la droite dans la poche de ma culotte.
> «Tu préfères pas les Lucky?» (13-14)

American chewing gum and cigarettes are part of a wider dream of the American way of life for Jo, part of his adolescent ambitions

now that he has emerged from the war. He can begin to live as an
individual rather than as someone whose destiny has been closely
related to the destiny of his country and his religion:

> La guerre est finie et le monde commence. De ce monde, je veux avoir
> ma part, et, tant qu'à faire, pas une petite. Je veux un gros morceau, un
> énorme. Comme sur les écrans... les types qu'ont des palaces, des
> Pontiac climatisées et des téléphones blancs avec une pépée dans
> chaque pièce en pyjama lamé. (14)

It is a dream closely associated with Hollywood cinema. He
makes frequent mention of American film stars, for example
Bogart; George Raft, James Cagney and Abbott and Costello; Errol
Flynn; John Wayne; Pat O'Brien; and Gary Cooper (18; 134; 146;
200; 204; 220). Jo now has American sporting heroes to emulate,
for example the boxer Rocky Marciano (136). These outweigh the
references to French icons. Jacques Hélian, the French band leader
and singer, is mentioned, but it is in the context of his 1944 «C'est
une fleur de Paris» (88), which is a patriotic song about how Paris
can now live again after the war, rather like Jo. Even the popular
French singer Georges Ulmer (who was actually born in Norway)
sings songs about cowboys in the Far West on the Saint-Granier
show (42). Old worries about textile and clothes rationing are
replaced with the dream of the new-look dresses, the fashion
introduced by Christian Dior in 1947 (88). No mention is made of
the hostile reaction to the extravagant use of material from a public
with the experience of deprivation.

It is therefore the idealised vision of a new world and a new
future that counts for Jo in *Baby-foot* rather than the actual French
context. This is far from the life-threatening real historical, political
and social context of *Un sac de billes*. At the very end of the novel, in
an Epilogue, Joffo describes the oral examination part of his 'certif'.
The examiner is the father of his old enemy Fouloche. He does not
want to hear Jo's answers to questions on the geography or history
of France. While this is his way of making amends for the past, it
may also be seen as symbolic of a change in attitude away from the

realities of everyday life. Indeed, he awards Jo an exceptionally high eighteen out of twenty, and then Jo returns home to discover a cake is being baked in celebration of his success, or as consolation for his failure. It is eaten hot, rather than being allowed to cool down as normal, while his plans for the future are being discussed.

# The question of identity

## Identity and the self

Jo, aged ten at the beginning of *Un sac de billes* and fourteen at the beginning of *Baby-foot*, develops from childhood to early adolescence, surrounded by older members of his family, his friends and the sets of different communities in which he finds himself. His character and its development are an integral part of the two works, his own perceptions of his identity and character being set in the context of his experiences with others and how they react to him.

He begins *Un sac de billes* demonstrating his unbounding optimism and confidence in himself. His favourite marble makes him feel like a giant, with the whole world in his pocket (**9**). It is a talisman that will enable him to succeed, even when all appears to be lost, as he states that he will use this 'planète miniature' to regain all the marbles he has lost in the game with his brother (**11**). Yet, even here, at the very outset, his confidence is shaded by an adult-like concern and care for others. He loves the marble for the confidence it gives him, but he is also aware that it is not because it is the biggest or the best. It is 'la plus moche de toutes' (**9**). The reader can sense from the outset that he will develop into an adolescent and adult who will match self-confidence with compassion for others.

Indeed, his development tends to be along a path set between contrasting positive and negative aspects of his character. On the positive side he shows initiative, courage, intelligence and creativity. These are mirrored by their negative aspects, initiative being also foolhardiness and rashness, courage being also the aggression he finds in boxing. In *Un sac de billes* Jo is quick to show initiative whenever he is a difficult situation. The examples range from the merely uncomfortable to the critical. It is he who, after attending to the blister on his foot without worrying his elder brother about it, arranges the lift with the comte de V. to enable them to continue the journey (**68-70**). At the Gare Saint-Charles in Marseille, he is quick to lie to the police, to realise that he must ignore Maurice, and to find a 'father' to prevent their arrest (**82-84**). At the Hôtel Excelsior he intervenes in the interrogation, answering in place of Maurice a question about their Jewish identity (**159**). He displays courage when he tells Maurice not to return if his brother cannot find 'proof' of their Catholicism, saying it is better for one to escape than for two to die (**175**). He is ready to attack the Excelsior interpreter on the station at Cannes if he causes them any trouble (**189**). At the end of the novel, he wants to join the *maquis* as soon as he hears about it (**208**).

Such initiative generally has positive results in *Un sac de billes*, enabling himself and others to survive in critical situations, but similar episodes in *Baby-foot* tend to relate to more mundane events, for example putting his socks over his shoes to prevent them slipping on the ice and risking the cart laden with black market chewing gum crashing down the hill (49-50). This is introduced by the statement: 'Il faut savoir prendre des risques', but the risks are not of the same scale as in *Un sac de billes*. Even there, Jo's desire to join the *maquis* is not actually for his survival, but to impress Françoise. Jo's displays of initiative are thus sometimes not far removed from his displays of rashness and spontaneity, usually associated with fighting others. He is the one who starts fights with his brother (**17**), and, a few pages later is the one to lash out in the playground after being called 'Youpin' (**26**). It is to lead in *Baby-foot* to his interest in boxing and the lesson he is taught, making him realise that boxing is a cruel sport (131).

He is intelligent and creative. We learn that he began reading at an early age (**19**), and continued to be a passionate reader, finishing two or three books a day while recuperating after his breakdown in Nice (**173**). However, it is his creativity that causes trouble in Vallauris when he asks to be able to make a pot according to his own design (**141-2**). He learns from experience, sometimes quickly, sometimes quite slowly as with the boxing. He develops a set of moral values, for example that fighting never serves a useful purpose (85), that lying does not always work (136-7). Alongside this he begins to develop an awareness of the power of painting, saying how little he understood of the *Mona Lisa*, but appreciated the movement he could perceive in the painting of Moretti (100-1).

Jo has a strong sense of belonging to his family, especially in *Un sac de billes*. He has a realistic love / hate relationship with his brother Maurice that shadows his development towards individuality. At the beginning of *Un sac de billes* he explains that brotherly love is one brother giving back the marble he has just won from the other brother (**10**), and he does not want to be seen crying by Maurice (**16**). There is an easy family relationship when he and Maurice arrive at Menton and meet the elder brothers Henri and Albert. Henri and Albert's first comments are identical, displaying evidence of a close, shared family experience and family language, both of them saying: '«Ho, ho, voilà les voyous»' (**87-88**). Their shared family experience encompasses the stories of their family's ancestors. Gradually, however, the influence of the family becomes less strong as Jo develops. He does not want to be seen to resemble his brother Maurice at the end of *Un sac de billes* because this would encroach on his individuality (**196**), and, in *Baby-foot*, he admits that he is growing apart from his family, getting on better with his friends than with them (20), and that he is not able to bear the way his mother fusses over him (43). Later in the same novel he states that he is now growing apart even from his old friends, preferring new experiences such as meeting girls (97). Even though the final scene of *Baby-foot* is a family meal, it is clear that the family ties have changed in character. Jo has moved away from them and the small community they represented as he experienced new contexts as part of the realistic process of growing up.

Jo is the only character to be fully developed in either work. As perhaps is natural and realistic in works about a child's development from childhood to adolescence, the other characters, even those who play a significant role in his life, such as Maurice in *Un sac de billes*, or Franck, Jeannot and Greenbaum in *Baby-foot*, tend to function in relation to Jo's world rather than as individuals within their own. His mother and father serve as symbols of a close-knit, traditional family. Jo's father is the one who is the central formative influence on Jo, the one who has given him the love of storytelling, and a sense of belonging to a past. The father is the one who prepares Jo and Maurice for the trials ahead before they leave, conscious of what has happened to the family in the past. He is always outwardly strong and optimistic, though Jo states that when he and Maurice left Paris, he remained 'les yeux fermés, berçant une douleur immémoriale' (**35**). By the end of the work he has changed status. He is more than Jo's father, he becomes representative of the Jews in World War Two and in history, suffering and dying because of his faith.

Compared to his father, Jo's mother plays a much more minor role. She seems much weaker, more stereotypically female, for example when she helps them to dress before they leave Paris. She is seen as unable to do more than help them automatically while bathed in tears. Ironically she is very similar to the type of wife-mother that the Pétain government advocated. Equally, Henri and Albert are only sketchily developed. Their role is to function as older brothers, but perhaps more importantly, they serve to symbolise the strength of the family ties when Jo and Maurice join them. Finally it might be argued that Maurice, were he not to exist, would need to be invented. He acts as a foil for Jo, the person who gives Jo a sense of security and who enables Jo to engage in realistic dialogue about what is happening. He enables the story to proceed in a dynamic way rather than an overly introspective way, just as Don Quixote needed a solid Sancho Panza.

Overall, therefore, Jo is the central character of both works. His family acts primarily as a symbolic of the values that Joffo wishes to support, as well as a reminder of Jo's Jewishness and his Jewish past. They enable him to realise the importance of his religion and culture at a particular time: 'Cette histoire me colle à la peau, elle fait partie intégrante de ce que je suis: un juif à part entière, qui a payé pour cela!' (**244**). But the lessons he learns and wishes to transmit are those of self-reliance. Faced with the real problems of growing up, he has to rely on himself rather than on others, and so it is not surprising that others take second place to him:

Il s'agissait aussi de transmettre à mes enfants un témoignage, une expérience et des valeurs que je crois essentielles. Être courageux, se débrouiller, ne compter sur personne... (**248**)

## Identity as 'otherness'

The characters not only have a personal identity as perceived by themselves, they are also selves as perceived by others. Jo develops not only as an individual self, but also develops in relation to wider groups such as his family, his friends and, in particular, Jews: His identity shifts and changes depending on where he situates himself at a particular moment and how the different groups to which he belongs perceive him. He therefore develops not only a personal identity, but social ones.

Such a set of identities is normal in any society, but it becomes a significant feature, especially in *Un sac de billes* where Jo has to adapt to acutely different group expectations while at the same time developing his own particular identity. This also reflects the general condition of any person growing up in France, accorded rights and freedoms as an individual by the state, but which the state then prescribes by the sets of duties and obligations which it expects of the French citizen. *Un sac de billes* sharpens this dual perspective on individual identity, not only for Jo but for the whole of the French nation, by showing how individuals react when placed suddenly into the very different political and cultural context of occupation by Nazi Germany and / or Pétain's 'État Français'. Alongside this is another context within which Jo must grow up, that of being a Jew. As Krausz and Tulea state:

On a structural and symbolic level, it is essential for Jews, for their own perception of themselves as Jews and for their perception by non-Jews, to have at their disposal a global structure of interpretation of the Jewish condition, that helps understand why it is legitimate for Jews, no matter where they live or come from and whether they travel or not, to perceive themselves as being simultaneously here and there; as being simultaneously part of a universal present shared with all the world, and part of a history, equally distant from myth and utopia,

which they share with their brother Jews. It is essential for Jews to
have it clear in mind that the specificity of the Diaspora/Jewish
condition enjoins Jews to be involved, though on distinct levels, in
many historical experiences simultaneously: that of their own people
and that of the nations. (*4*, pp. 24-25)

The specific issue of Jews in France, as outlined in the Introduction,
adds further to Jo's complexity, especially in *Un sac de billes*. Jo is an
individual, but he is also a Jew who began life in republican France,
and who then lives in a France occupied by Nazi Germany.

At the heart of Jo's life, particularly at the beginning, is his family.
A formative influence on any child, the family has special
connotations for Jews, as Isidore Epstein writes:

In no other religion has the duty of the parents to instruct their
children been more stressed than in Judaism; much less has it
anywhere else occupied such a central position. Many of the religious
precepts have been especially ordained for the express purpose of
educating the children. (*5*, p. 197)

The educational influence of the family is paralleled by that of the
past. The events of Jewish history can act as models to shape
current action (*5*, p. 148). Jo is therefore not only himself and a
member of a family; he is more specifically a member of a Jewish
family with a strong sense of family history. He is a young child
who needs protecting, as would be a function of any strong family
unit. Jo recognises this in *Baby-foot* when he states that he wants to
be himself, but his that mother protects him too much because he is
her youngest child: 'Je suis le petit dernier, évidemment. Elle veut
me couver. Mais, tout de même, j'aimerais qu'elle me laisse vivre ma
vie' (43). As a Jewish child, however, his family needs to make him
aware of his religion, his past, and the predicament in which the
family now finds itself. At its extreme his mother and father see him
as someone who needs to be taught to lie about his Jewishness for
his own safety (**33-34**), and, as part of the lesson, he is slapped by
his father to try to make him say that he is a Jew. The normal
protective and caring atmosphere is in which he is able to develop

as a child and as a Jew is changed into one in which he is not able to be himself, having to submit to the greater value of the continuation of the Jewish family.

In another family he would have a family identity different from that which he perceives as his own. This happens when he stays with the Manceliers, who assume that he is not Jewish and treat him as such. He cannot be freely himself within this family group either. When, however, he is with the Compagnons de France, another form of 'family' unit, he is more free to be himself since he is able to do what he wants, but again within limitations:

> Le soir, les veillées se raccourcissent, une méfiance s'est installée. Mais même ainsi, ce camp est pour moi le paradis, il est bon d'aller où bon vous semble, et surtout d'être à l'air. (**184**)

## Stereotyping of the self by the Other

The family unit is only one of the groups in which Jo finds himself. While he sees his Jewish family as being 'normal' in that it he is able to develop within its space, other groupings are based on 'abnormality' when the group identity is so categorised by others for political or other reasons that the personal self risks being obliterated. For Jo, as with so many others, this is what happened with the categorisation of Jewishness, leading to a stereotyping that denied real identity. Jo is very aware of this at the beginning of *Un sac de billes* when, after being forced to wear the yellow star denoting his Jewishness, he says:

> Mais qu'est-ce qui vient d'arriver? J'étais un gosse, moi, avec des billes, des taloches, des cavalcades, des jouets, des leçons à apprendre, papa était coiffeur, mes frères aussi, maman faisait la cuisine, le dimanche papa nous emmenait à Longchamp voir les canassons et prendre l'air, la semaine en classe et voilà tout, et tout d'un coup on me colle quelques centimètres carrés de tissu et je deviens juif. (**23**)

This short statement shows his awareness of how his own identity as a child has existed alongside and within other natural groups such as his family or school, but how now he will be seen by others not as an individual, nor even as a member of one of the natural groups to which he belonged previously, but as a member of a single group—the Jews. The danger is that this group, one to which he had belonged before alongside others, is not only to be the only group to which others see him belonging, but also its identity has been fixed by stereotyping. Immediately after the above quotation, Jo describes a propaganda poster depicting the Jew as a spider, with the legend that Jews are trying to take over the world. He comments that, when he had seen the poster previously, he had not taken any notice of it since he had not associated the image with himself or Jewishness. Now he realises that others will perceive him through this image, reducing his identity not even to the Jewish one that was part of his heritage, but to a stereotypical, false one:

> On passait souvent devant avec Maurice. Ça nous faisait ni chaud ni froid, c'etait pas nous ce monstre! On n'était pas des araignées et on n'avait pas une tête pareille, Dieu merci; j'étais blondinet, moi, avec les yeux bleus et un pif comme tout le monde. Alors, c'était simple: le Juif n'était pas moi.
>
> Et voilà tout d'un coup, cet abruti me disait que j'avais un tarin [nose] comme sur l'affiche! Tout ça parce que j'avais une étoile. ( 24)

Joffo explores not only the dangers of stereotyping, but also how its false exaggeration is readily undermined by people refusing to accept it as pertaining to the real world, or inadvertently not recognising the stereotype. Early in *Un sac de billes*, Jo asks his father what a Jew is, but his father cannot find an answer (**34**). As a Jew, Jo's father does not perceive his own Jewish identity as a simplistic one, and certainly does not recognise any relationship between it and the stereotypical image offered by their contemporary society. Another similar example is that offered by Joffo in his 'Dialogue avec mes lecteurs', where he quotes the Catholic priest who saved Jo and Maurice on the train. The priest saw them both as 'children' in danger rather than as 'Jewish children', and saved them (**234-5**).

An ironic example of the undermining of stereotyping is given when two German SS officers go into the family barber's shop at the beginning. They are unaware that the barber's is Jewish, and perceive Jo and Maurice as children, not Jews. They therefore look on them with a kindness that would be totally inappropriate if they had perceived them as Jewish children (13). Conversely, Simon Rauschenburger, whom Henri and Albert had seen on a train, is an orthodox Catholic, and not Jewish as the German policeman had suspected from his stereotypically Jewish name (88-89). Further examples of the undermining of stereotypes are the comment by Jo that the SS soldiers speak French with less of an accent than many in the quarter (13), and that the German language is very similar to the Yiddish language spoken by Jews (43).

The wider issues of the relationship between stereotyping and propaganda are also explored. Jo and Maurice go to a cinema in Marseille where they watch a news film produced by the Nazis that projects only the most grandiose and sublime aspects of France for propaganda purposes. It is followed by *Les Aventures du Baron de Munchausen* [*sic*] (75). Josef Goebbels, Reichsminister of propaganda and also chief of the German UFA film studios, had ordered this film to be made for the twenty-fifth anniversary of the UFA in 1943. Jo comments that, even though the film was a propaganda one, it delighted the two of them, and thus the propaganda failed in its purpose (80). Similarly Jo is very aware of the falseness of propaganda by any side in the war when he is able to compare a newspaper report about Stalingrad produced by the Germans to a report on the same battle on Radio Londres (118-9). He does not know which one to believe.

These are all lessons for Jo, experiences which play a role in forming his identity. They even influence his perception of his own self-confidence and inclination towards rashness in coming to conclusions when he himself falls into the trap of stereotyping another person. At Jo and Maurice's sister Rosette's house in Ainay-le-Vieil, there is a discussion about the dangers of denunciation by others in the village. An old women enters the house, appears to be delaying her departure, and asks pointed questions about Jo and

Maurice. Jo immediately suspects her of being ready to denounce them to the Germans, but is proven wrong: she too is a Jew, living under a false name in the village. As Jo comments: 'La carrière de détective privé que j'envisage depuis trois minutes vient de s'éloigner de moi à tout jamais' (**198**).

Once the war is over, however, he appears to have forgotten the lesson. In *Baby-foot* he becomes dazzled by stereotypical identities, seeing them as role models to be emulated in his own development. The stereotypes are, however, of a different nature, being much more similar to the aspirations of any fourteen-year-old child. He is attracted to the glamour of America, in particular Hollywood, and to the legends of the boxing ring. It could be argued that the Jo of *Baby-foot* is himself a stereotype of an adolescent with unattainable idols. He seems to lead a much more one-dimensional existence than in *Un sac de billes*, and the lessons he learns concerning stereotypes are more straightforward and personal. When he learns that Greenbaum has not led a glamorous life in America, he is amazed, but, rather than forget the stereotype of America, he transforms Greenbaum into 'notre Amerlo' (31), separating him from the stereotype. He only completely articulates his rejection of stereotypes at the end of the novel when talking to his brother Henri, offering to work as a barber alongside him:

> Je l'aime bien, mon frangin râleur. C'est dur à dire quand on a voulu être Al Capone, Joe Louis, Zorro et Rockefeller en même temps, mais c'est peut-être lui qui a raison.
> «Je ne sais pas trop, je pourrais peut-être te filer un coup de main au salon.»
> Je hoche la tête avec plus d'énergie.
> «Oui, c'est ça, je vais travailler au salon.» (218)

Incidentally, some Joffos are still to be found working as barbers in Paris. Brother Henri is still, at the age of eighty-five, to be found at the spacious premises on the appropriately-named rue du 8 mai 1945, just opposite the Gare de l'Est, and one of Joseph's nephews, Robby, runs a salon-cum-antique shop in the rue du Laos (XV$^e$).

## Identity and space

As is seen above, the characters have different identities depending on the context or group in which they find themselves. It is more complex than the obvious difference between being the member of one religion or nation against as opposed to another one—or even, at a different level, being a member of one football team as opposed to another one, or a supporter of the Racing rather than the Red Star side (53-54). It is an issue that permeates, in particular, *Un sac de billes*, a work about belonging or not belonging to a space, and the barriers between spaces as the characters either cross from one to the other or are made aware of the presence of the other from the space in which they find themselves. As they locate themselves in one space they are aware of their identity within that space, and are aware at the same time of how their identity might be different if set outside that space. This structure closely follows the 'rites of passage' structure as proposed by Turner in *The Ritual Process* (2, p. 94), in which the individual is first separated from his normal social space, enters a period of liminality or marginality, a space that is like neither the previous space nor the one to be entered in the third phase which is the reintegration of the individual into a stable space once more. It could be argued that *Un sac de billes* focuses on the first two of these stages, while *Baby-foot* focuses on the move from the stage of liminality to final integration. As Turner writes: 'Liminal entities are neither here nor there; they are betwixt and between the positions assigned and arrayed by law, custom, convention and ceremonial' (2, p. 95). Jo and Maurice are in a social limbo in which they lose the attributes of their previous status, for example their family history and their distinctive religion. They have no possessions (2, p. 95) and become 'invisible'. Turner, in *From Ritual to Theatre* (3, p. 25), also indicates that the liminal period may involve a geographical movement, a symbolic crossing of thresholds separating different areas before final reintegration into society. It is clear that this echoes more strongly the plight of Jo and Maurice as they proceed across France than the experiences of Jo in *Baby-foot*.

There is another difference between the two works. *Un sac de billes* could represent two different versions of this rites of passage. The novel describes not only how Jo moves from his original space, through sets of others, finally to be reintegrated in his original space, but also a parallel movement undertaken by the French nation. The French were forced to leave their republican context, enter a new space 'occupied' by the Germans or the 'unoccupied' space of the new French State, attempt to work out their new identity within these spaces before finally being reintegrated into a new French space after Liberation. *Baby-foot* does not have such a strong dual structure. As stated earlier, it is more akin to a *roman d'éducation*, focusing on the final stages of Jo's move out of liminality to the end of childhood and the entry into adulthood. It is the story of a character who undergoes a series of adventures that form his character and afford him a more mature view of himself and of the world he is in. A typical *roman d'éducation* involves an opposition between the aspirations of the main character and the limitations on those aspirations which are imposed by or on him in the light of the wider needs of society and his or her realisation of weaknesses. The experience teaches the character sets of lessons, and the former aspirations or illusions become modified.

## a) Closed spaces: security versus insecurity

Given the importance of the movement across and between spaces in the structure of the rites of passage, it is significant that *Un sac de billes*, in particular, has so many examples of them, especially closed spaces, separated in some way from their surrounding space(s). These spaces may be significant and political such as those of Occupied and Unoccupied France, or the seemingly trivial and personal ones. Both have connotations of safety, security and the freedom to be one's self on the one hand, and on the other hand lack of security and limitations to this freedom. Unoccupied France appears to offer security once Jo and Maurice have crossed the demarcation line, but its space is as life-threatening as that of Occupied France. On a more personal level of incident within the insecure space of Occupied France, when Jo and Maurice are under the blankets behind the closed door of their bedroom in the dark at the beginning of *Un sac de billes*, Jo comments: 'On est bien sous les couvertures, des voix étouffées nous parviennent puis se taisent. C'est une nuit comme toutes les nuits, une nuit de 1941' (**20**).

Despite the insecurity of the world around them in the France of 1941, they are safe, and yet are still aware of what is happening outside their spacial safety. Later, after they have crossed the line, Jo is able to sleep in security under the blankets behind the closed door of the farmhouse bedroom. However, the outside threats are still there as he realises an hour later when he discovers that Maurice has disappeared (**60-61**). Other examples work in the same way. In the closed space of the forest as they cross the demarcation line they are superficially safe since they have a guide, but they sense threats all around them (**57**). The space of the Compagnons de France camp offers protection behind its gate (**134-5**); the darkened cinema in Marseille offers them an escape from the real world into the fantasy world of Baron von Münchhausen. Perhaps the most interesting example is when Jo and Maurice board the train to leave Paris at the beginning. They feel secure since they have managed to board the train and are within the closed space of the carriage, but a sense of insecurity is created when the train leaves the station. Jo does not realise that their train is moving. He sees only a neighbouring train going towards the station, an impossibility since it was already at the terminus. He has experienced a phenomenological moment, in which the world is seen not through any framework of connotations or interpretations, but as it 'is', perceived from the viewpoint of pure experience. It is a moment of real freedom, denoting that Jo, albeit for a very short time, is free from a world whose meaning has been changed by historical and political events outside his control.

There are other moments of freedom associated with closed spaces, but again they are temporary and usually associated with some idea of threat. At the beginning of the novel, for example, Jo and Maurice's father allows them not to return to school but to have an afternoon of freedom. Jo had already sensed a growing feeling of exclusion within the school space, and now possesses the open streets of Paris:

> Tout un après-midi à nous, alors que les autres travailleraient! C'était bien fait pour eux, ils nous avaient exclus eh bien c'était à notre tour de les posséder, pendant qu'ils moisiraient sur les problèmes et les participes passés, nous on prendrait un grand coup de sirop de la rue, le meilleur sirop des meilleures rues, les rues de notre royaume. ( **28**)

Conversely, at the very end of the novel, Jo describes at length the great efforts he had to make to board the train for Paris. He had to create the space by sheer physical effort, his body being initially horizontal within the closed space of the carriage. He is in control of this space, despite the attempts by those around him not to let him occupy it, and this time he knows he is moving towards freedom. Joffo significantly ends this passage with a series of dots across the page, suggesting openness and the offer to the reader or Jo to fill in the gaps as they wish (**226-7**), a freedom that was denied in the controlled spaces of the rest of the novel.

The wider context of political, social and even metaphysical connotations that is an integral part of the closed spaces of *Un sac de billes* is largely absent from *Baby-foot*. Closed spaces do occur, but they are less frequent. They are often associated with a dual significance of security and insecurity, but, as stated above, they are related to Jo's development towards adulthood rather than being integrated into the history of France. Jo is free to choose to enter the closed spaces in which his freedom becomes threatened, rather than being forced to enter them to save his life. When he has to escape Bernadette's bedroom and becomes 'imprisoned' on the balcony, (155-9), it is related to his sexual development and the personal lessons he must learn. Equally he is free to choose to enter the boxing ring, another set of closed spaces that will lead to more self-knowledge. At the end of the work, the episode most similar to those of *Un sac de billes* occurs when he is trapped inside the lorry driven by Boydt towards Berlin, but again the episode, while worrying for him, is merely another episode from which he needs to escape. As he says after the Bernadette episode, he is learning about himself:

> Les yeux ouverts dans le noir, je me dis que les échecs s'accumulent. Le trafic, la boxe, l'amour et les chemins de la gloire sont encore bien loin. [...] Je me demande si je ne vais pas devoir réenvisager mes positions...
>     Qui vivra verra. (161)

### b) The boundaries between spaces

In *Un sac de billes*, the boundaries and frontiers between the spaces are of two kinds. On the one hand there are those that can be classed as political, social or cultural. On the other hand there are those associated with life-threatening or identity-changing events. The divisions are not clear-cut, however. A boundary that is social or cultural may also be based on political divisions and may also involve personal issues and identity. It is this complex interweaving of the global with the individual that is a significant quality of this work. *Baby-foot*, by contrast, tends to have boundaries that are associated with the individual, the frontiers that Jo must cross to move towards attaining maturity.

The clearest political boundary in *Un sac de billes* is the demarcation line between the Occupied and Unoccupied zones of France. This is the one that Jo and Maurice must cross to leave the space in which they have lived, but which is now controlled by the Germans (32-33), in order to enter the supposedly free space of 'France libre' (33). Once there they will go to Menton, geographically as far from the demarcation line as possible, next to the Italian frontier (33). The line, while figurative in the sense that it divided occupation from freedom, is also present politically since Jo and Maurice need papers to cross it. In the event, however, the line is not visible—as they expect it to be: 'Nous foulons le pavé de

Dax, la France libre n'est pas loin. On passera' (**47**), and they cross
it without realising they have done so. Jo has a sense of frustration
that somehow he has been prevented from achieving a goal, of
pitting himself against the life-threatening forces of massed German
patrols:

> Le sentiment qui s'est d'abord emparé de moi a été la frustration. On
> avait passé la ligne et je ne m'en étais pas aperçu! Il y avait ce but à
> atteindre, on était partis pour ça, tout le monde en parlait, c'était le
> bout du monde, et moi sans m'en douter j'étais passé comme une
> fleur, totalement inconscient, à travers ce trait de crayon qui coupait
> en deux la carte de France que papa nous avait montrée un soir.
>      La ligne! Je me l'imaginais comme un mur, un espace bourré de
> guérites, de canons, de mitrailleuses, de barbelés, avec des patrouilles
> se faufilant dans la nuit avec des grands coups de projecteurs fouillant
> chaque brin d'herbe. (**58**)

In effect he has been denied an experience that might have led to
the testing of his courage—one aspect of his personal
development—but he does learn a lesson about the fallibilty of
political symbols, the demarcation line not being in practice what
propaganda had led him to believe. In this incident it is Maurice
who learns an immediate personal lesson. He sees that it is easy to
cross the line and does so eight times with groups of refugees,
earning the money they both need to continue their journey (**64-65**).
The political nature of barriers is further explored in references to
the barriers that other characters encounter, for example Ange Testi
who is forced to remain in France, unable to return to Algiers from
his holiday in France since the Americans landed in North Africa
(**138**). However, the connotation of undermining is rarely far from
his consciousness. Jo sees how the Italians, initially on the side of
the Germans, are forced to return behind their frontier after the
armistice, this time to fight against the Germans (**132**). Yet another
barrier is set up outside the family barber's shop at the beginning of
the work. The Germans have placed a sign—«Yiddish Geschefb»—
outside, turning the family workspace into a political space. The two
SS soldiers who enter the space are not aware that they have

crossed a barrier. The sign is hidden and so they enter unawares. Nevertheless, even when undermined, the threat of the barrier or frontier is still real. The characters' lives are controlled by the barriers they encounter, and they have to live according to the space in which they find themselves, ready to adapt when the barriers change.

The symbol of the barrier is not only reflected in the lives of those in *Un sac de billes*. It is part of the history of Jo's family, who had to flee across the frontiers of many countries before finally crossing into France. Significantly they too do not realise that they have arrived in France until they see the motto of France on a building. They, like Jo, knew where they were going, but arrived without realising it (**19**).

The same ambiguities are seen with the other frontiers of a more general kind. The man on the station at Marseille becomes Jo's 'father' without realising it, crossing from one identity to another unawares (**84**). Jo thinks that he has crossed the line between childhood and adulthood when he has to leave Paris at the beginning (**30**). While it may be the frontier between one type of childhood and the move towards adulthood, he is still in effect a child who will develop towards adulthood in this work and in *Baby-foot*.

The lesson is that it is not the significant frontiers that create danger, it is the apparently insignificant ones that do so. *Un sac de billes* reflects the absurd world of the twentieth century where the locus of meaning is not necessarily clear. Rather like Sartre's Roquentin in *La Nausée*, who experiences an awakening to the full potential of life in front of a tree root, or Sarraute's insignificant *tropisme* movements that may signify aggression and fear, Jo realises that it is the small incidents that are the most significant. Meeting two policemen, he lifts his beret politely:

> Ce geste, et peut-être le fait que je me sois lavé les mains et le visage dans le lavabo des toilettes, le fait aussi que je me sois mis de l'eau sur les cheveux et repeigné en me faisant la raie droite, a pu jouer en ma faveur. Il y a des moments où il suffit de peu de chose pour que la vie continue ou qu'elle s'arrête. (**82**)

In *Baby-foot*, the frontiers and boundaries work differently. Whereas *Un sac de billes* is based on sets of spaces, each bounded and closed in some way one from the other as part of a single yet complex context, that of wartime France, *Baby-foot* sets the development of Jo as a linear progression between two distinct spaces, that of post-war France and that of America. The former is real but offers limitations and constraints; the latter is illusory, but is open. Jo moves from one space to another, each being represented by separate incidents and events. Jo discovers that he does not wish to become a boxer either in the small-time rings of France or in the illusory world of America; he has his first sexual encounter that ends, not as it might have done in Hollywood or as Romeo with his Juliet, but with ignominious flight (160). There is no sense that the incidents are linked one to the other by any other necessity than chronology. The sequencing could equally be different, there being no necessity that one should take place before another, or that the spaces coincide in any meaningful way. As Jo says at the end of his journey with Boydt, the only means of continuing the journey forward is by hitch-hiking (211). There is no specificity in the means to the end, only the end point, the lesson learnt. This is underpinned by the way in which the majority of the chapters end, with an aphorism demonstrating an aim desired (71; 102; 111), or a lesson learnt (131; 161; 220), or by an incomplete statement shown by series of dots (16; 60; 140) breaking the link with the succeeding chapter.

### Identity and game-playing

On a different level of individual and group identities are the different types of game or sport that the characters play. The titles of the two works denote the central role that game-playing has, and the content covers many other games and sports beyond marbles and table football. The theoretical implications of play were explored in detail by Huizinga (6). While others have elaborated on his theories, in particular Ehrmann, Lewis and Lewis (7), the essence of Huizinga's ideas remain relevant to a discussion of the role of play in these works:

> Summing up the formal characteristics of play we might call it a free activity standing quite consciously outside 'ordinary' life as being 'not serious', but at the same time absorbing the player intensely and utterly. It is an activity connected with no material interest, and no profit can be gained by it. It proceeds within its own proper boundaries of time and space according to fixed rules and in an orderly manner. It promotes the formation of social groupings which tend to surround themselves with secrecy and to stress their difference from the common world by disguise or other means. ( 6, p. 13)

It is therefore an activity associated with freedom, since the player knows that he has stepped outside 'normal' life with its 'normal' obligations and constraints, and outside the 'normal' location and time. Play occurs in a world with its own rules that are either the agreed rules of the group playing or the invented rules of the individual. Even for the individual there is often a group aspect in that the game may be a traditional one, or, for language games, may play with the 'group' language. Huizinga includes organised sports with play, but indicates that any development towards professionalism takes sport out of the realm of play, and the quality of freedom is lost (6, p. 197).

It is also an activity closely linked to war. This adds to the denseness of *Un sac de billes*, since Jo and Maurice play games freely outside their 'normal life', but their 'normal' life is one in which different populations are at war. Huizinga puts war formally into the category of play, albeit an extreme form, because it is a form of competition bound by rules of behaviour. However, he adds the rider that war can only be regarded in this way:

> ... so long as it is waged within a sphere whose members regard each other as equals or antagonists with equal right; in other words its cultural function depends on its play-quality. This condition changes as soon as war is waged outside the sphere of equals, against groups not recognised as human beings, and thus deprived of human rights—

barbarians, devils, heathens, heretics and 'lesser breeds without the law'. (*6*, pp. 89-90)

Such a distinction is very relevant to the war situation in which Jo and Maurice find themselves, since they, as Jews, are not treated as equals by the Germans. An extension to this link between play and war is the argument of Plato, in his *Republic*, that play is an imitation of all reality. When children play, they imitate adult life around them, learning for example the leadership or team-working skills that they will need in adulthood. Play is educational in the broadest sense. Games appear on the surface not to relate to the outside world because they are acted out in a separate time and place but, because they are associated to the individual and the skills that can be displayed and developed within the rules of the game and the aspirations of the team or other player(s), they teach children how best to operate once they are adults.

The games in the two works are of various kinds, symbolised by their titles. They are significant in Huizingian terms because of their connotations of freedom, space and shared rules of conduct. They are also educational in the Platonic sense. Jo can play out in controlled conditions actions equivalent to those which in real life can lead to tragedy and death. Marbles are important for Jo in *Un sac de billes* not only because playing marbles symbolises the childhood he feels he is leaving by the end (**198**), but also because playing with them tests out reaction, behaviour and other strategies, and thus prepares him for the responsibly competitive nature of adulthood. Marbles is a spontaneous game with individuals capturing another's possessions, and is paralleled on a more organized team level by football (52-54). As Jo says here, however, he is not 'un fan du foot'. He prefers the more spontaneous games he plays with his friends, the games frequently symbolizing a sense of freedom, for example on the beach at Menton when he and Maurice have safely met up with their elder brothers: 'Nous avons couru, sauté, dansé, crié, nous étions ivres de joie et de liberté. Cette fois-ci, ça y était, nous l'avions retrouvée, cette sacrée liberté' (**89**). Later there are the football games at R[umilly] once Jo has been accepted by the other children there. Their initial animosity disappears when they see Jo working in the town, and he is allowed to play with them, participating in a shared social activity (**208-9**).

The table football of *Baby-foot* has the same qualities as Jo's games of marbles. While it involves competitiveness between groups of people, it is a more spontaneous activity than organized team matches, being played in a café as part of a shared social activity. Even here, however, Jo is very aware of the warlike implications of table-football. It involves 'de la tactique, un lent travail de sape' and 'la chance tourne, juste comme je peux entrevoir la victoire' (22-23). Even more warlike is football since it can lead to extreme behaviour. Jo comments in *Baby-foot* that it is the difference between the teams that counts, as in politics: 'Le foot, c'est un peu come la politique. Ce qui compte, ce sont les extrêmes' (54).

Of the other games mentioned, childhood fights come very close to reflecting the actual historical situation. In *Un sac de billes*, Jo says that he is ready for 'une bataille forcenée' with his brother (**17**), and in *Baby-foot* he takes fighting onto another level with his interest in boxing. He is nicknamed 'Battling' by his brother Henri (104), a reference not only to the battles of war, but also to the common nickname for boxers, for example the Jewish American boxer Battling Levinsky. He becomes aware, however, that boxing changes the boxer. Jo's courage and resourcefulness in the face of adversity become pure uncontrolled aggression expressed in terms appropriate to an invading army or natural destructive force: 'En avant: je pars en crochets larges, dévastateurs, je demolish la Bretagne: la rade de Brest s'effondre, la pointe du Raz s'engloutit; adieu Paimpol et sa falaise…(125).

Above all, Jo enjoys playing for the sake of playing. It enables him to operate within his own space rather than in the space of others, especially at moments when his own space and his own freedom are under threat. For example, he runs a race with Maurice while waiting for Raymond to take them across the line (**55**) and they both play at word games in the interval at the cinema in Marseille (**80**).

Isaac Bashevis Singer, the Jewish novelist who has written many works about the role of the holocaust in relation to life, summarises the metaphysical nature of games in life. His comments could relate very specifically to the adventures of Jo:

> Everything is a game—nationalism, materialism, even suicide [...]. Since we are sure of nothing and there is no evidence that the sun will rise tomorrow, play is the very essence of human endeavour, perhaps even the thing-in-itself. God is a player, the cosmos a playground. For years I have searched for a basis of ethics and gave up hope. Suddenly it became clear to me. The basis of ethics is man's right to play the games of his choice. I will not trample on your toys and you will not trample on mine. I won't spit on your idol and you will not spit on mine. (*8*, pp. 141-2)

# Narration and narrative structures

## Narration

The issues concerning the relationship between real events and the way they are represented (or re-presented) by a narrator are central to an understanding of these works. They include the issues of genre and form—whether the text is an objective, historical document, an autobiography, or a piece of fiction; narration—the nature of the narrator and his or her role in re-presenting the historical events; and readership—the person or persons for whom the narration is intended. The issues concerning narratorship will be examined in the first part of this chapter, and will be followed by an analysis of the way in which the chronological sequence of events—the *fabula*—are turned into a plot through organization into a particular form or structure, and the implications of this structuring on the different levels of reader. Mieke Bal summarises the issues thus:

> Whenever events are presented, they are always presented from within a certain 'vision'. A point of view is chosen, a certain way of seeing things, a certain angle, whether 'real' historical facts are concerned or fictitious events. It is possible to try and give an 'objective' picture of the facts. But what does that involve? An attempt to present only what is seen or is perceived in some other way. All comment is shunned and implicit interpretation is also avoided. Perception, however, is a psychological process, strongly dependent on the position of the perceiving body; a small child sees things in a totally different way from an adult, if only as far as measurements are concerned. [...] Perception depends on so many factors that striving for objectivity is pointless. To mention only a few factors: one's position with respect to the perceived object, the fall of the light, the distance, previous knowledge, psychological attitude towards the object; all this and more affects the picture one forms and passes on to others. In a story, elements of the fabula are presented in a certain way. We are confronted with a vision of the fabula. (*9*, p. 100)

### a) Joffo as an adult

The narrator of both works is Joffo himself. This simple
statement hides, however, a multitude of complexities since the
first-person narratorship covers not only Joffo as an adult and Jo as
a child, but also the particular focus of their narratorship at
particular points in the story—whether they are recounting the
story, standing back from the story to comment on the events, or
even making general statements about society and politics.

Joffo is clearly aware of the issues relating to narratorship. In *Un
sac de billes*, at the end of his convalescence, he goes to find the
nurse, Mlle Hauser, who has cared for him. He shifts from narrating
what actually happened to a passage of reflection about the issues
pertaining to narratorship, in particular the problem a narrator has
when faced with a major event but only has formulaic, clichéd or
over-used language at his or her disposal. He shifts further to an
imagined projection of Mlle Hauser's subsequent life before
returning to comment on the immediacy of the events of the past
on him as an adult:

> Je sortis, je ne la vis pas dans le petit bureau vitré qu'elle occupait
> d'ordinaire tout près de ma chambre et dans lequel nous avions
> bavardé si souvent. J'allais écrire: «je ne la revis jamais», mais je
> m'aperçois que cela fait de nombreuses fois que j'emploie cette
> formule. Hélas! elle convient une fois de plus. Où vous en êtes-vous
> allée, mademoiselle Hauser? Dans quel camp avez-vous débarqué, l'un
> de ces matins brouillardeux et froids de Pologne ou d'Allemagne
> orientale? Tant d'années ont passé, et pourtant je revois le clair visage
> penché sur moi, je sens les mains douces sur mon front, j'entends la
> voix:
> —Tu devrais lire un peu, Joseph, tu ne vas plus à l'école… ( **173-4**)

A similar passage of reflection on narratorship occurs towards
the end of the novel, when he considers which tense to use to
recount events:

> Je préfère raconter la suite au présent, cela rendra peut-être l'aventure
> plus anodine, lui retirera cette aura de sacré que confèrent les temps
> passés, de l'imparfait au passé simple. Le présent est le temps sans
> surprise, un temps ingénu, celui où l'on vit les choses comme elles
> arrivent, elles sont neuves encore et vivantes, c'est le temps de
> l'enfance, celui qui me convenait. (**204**)

Joffo is only too aware of the problems of expressing himself. In
*Baby-foot* he writes about his difficulty when asked to comment on
his interest in Moretti's painting: 'subitement je ne trouve plus mes
mots... Comme il est soudain difficile d'exprimer ce que je ressens,
je cherche, je cherche, mais ça ne vient pas' (100-1). In these
passages, Joffo is standing outside the text, commenting as an adult
writer on the problems of writing and expressing ideas in general.

Sometimes Joffo comments on the way he is recounting his
narrative in a more specific manner. He uses his current knowledge
to give an additional meaning to an event that had no significance at
the time, and uses this knowledge to compare the perception of the
adult to that of the child. When introducing Mme Viale at Menton,
he states his reaction of surprise as a child, and then gives his
mature reflection as an adult to explain his surprise (**94**). A few
pages later he again compares his mature reflection to that of a child
experiencing the events at first hand: 'Cela m'aurait causé une
douleur profonde si, en cet instant, j'avais su que je ne reviendrais
jamais à la maison des Viale et que je ne devais plus les revoir' (**97**).
A similar passage occurs when he learns that the schoolteacher who
made them sing the *Marseillaise* was a Resistance leader:

> Lorsque je lui racontais, papa s'étonnait et admirait qu'on nous fasse
> chanter des choses pareilles, un parent d'élève pouvait se plaindre aux
> autorités, le directeur pouvait avoir des ennuis... J'ignorais alors que
> ce n'était pas les ennuis qu'il pouvait craindre, cet homme maigre au
> pantalon trop haut était l'un des chefs du réseau de Résistance des
> Alpes-Maritimes. (**123**)

Sometimes, as above, the information adds political connotations
to the events. Sometimes it is to produce narrative tension,

demonstrating how, as a child, he did not have all the information at his disposal to react fully and appropriately to an event, for example, at the beginning: 'Je ne savais pas que d'ici quelques heures, je ne serais plus un enfant' (30), or when he says that his father suffered enormously at their departure from Paris: 'J'ai su plus tard, lorsque tout fut fini, que mon père était resté debout, se balançant doucement, les yeux fermés, berçant une douleur immémoriale' (35). Later, the threat posed by the Germans, while being understood by Jo at the time, is given its full force by the information that Jean Masso disappeared: 'Avant de descendre l'escalier de l'office, je me retourne: je vois la tête de Jean, souriante entre deux épaules. Je ne sais pas encore que je ne le reverrai jamais, que personne n'a jamais revu Jean Masso' (169). This is a comment on the exceptional events of World War Two. In *Baby-foot*, a similar comment relating to Jeannot is, however, more of a narrative closure, a move from one set of relationships to another as part of Jo's development through adolescence, signifying his growing awareness of how friendships change: 'Sterling, Béro, les gitans, la guitare de Saranne, les danses, les feux de camp, les boîtes à chaussures, tout ce qui s'était succédé, Jeannot que je ne verrai plus, Franck, le temps d'avant...' (219).

Such interventions by the adult Joffo render the narrative voice much more complex concerning the events. He also intervenes to comment on his character as a child, giving a personal depth in a Proustian way when evoking the scents of childhood (11), or, in a more normally autobiographical way when he comments on how good he was at learning as a child (11), and how much he loved the stories his father told: 'Les enfants aiment les histoires, on leur en lit, on leur en invente, mais pour moi ce fut différent. Le héros en était mon grand-père dont je pouvais voir dans le salon un daguerréotype sur cadre ovale' (17).

This quotation is interesting since it leads from the general to the specific. Many of the adult Joffo's comments concern general political, social and other issues which relate only indirectly to the works. At times they are the typical comments of an adult regretting the changes that have been made since childhood, for example lamenting the fact that children no longer wear berets (**77**). He states his preference for the chaotic world of his childhood rather than the planned urban environment in which they live today (**11-12**). He regrets the urban developments at Menton, conveniently forgetting that the building of blocks of flats enables other people to enjoy the town in which he lived: 'La ville a changé, paraît-il, on a construit des gratte-ciel comme sur toute la côte, des résidences, de nouvelles plages jusqu'à la frontière italienne et au-delà' (**86**). The phrase 'paraît-il' is significant here. He is working totally within reported knowledge rather than from the experience that forms the basis of his childhood adventures.

Sometimes his comments focus on political and other issues underpinning the events, for example the colonial attitude of the French in Algeria: 'J'ai appris par la suite que l'on pouvait en effet vivre en Algérie et ne pas connaître les Arabes' (**164**), or the politics of the relationship between the Catholic Church and the Gestapo during the war: 'Il aurait été évidemment très désagréable pour la Gestapo de voir l'épiscopat prendre officiellement position contre elle' (**181**). The reason he gives here is that there were still many Catholic believers, and the potential hostility of the Catholic Church if the Gestapo were to deport two children, forced the Gestapo to retain a form of neutrality.

### b) Joffo as a child

It is interesting to see how Jo, as a child, is already aware of the different levels of narration that he uses as an adult. While this does beg the question of how much the narrative of Jo as a child is authentic, and how much is constructed by Joffo as an adult, nevertheless, the freshness of much of his comments as a child do strike as original memories by the adult Joffo of how he actually felt as a child.

Many statements are based on speculations concerning language, the ways in which events can be expressed. When they are embedded into an incident, they are probably a real memory of what happened. For example when he comments on his linguistic discovery that Parmesans were people too: 'Je les connais tous, il y a [...] un charpentier parmesan (je croyais avant de le connaître que les Parmesans étaient uniquement des fromages)' (115). A similar episode occurs when Jo meets the comte de V., and calls the cart 'un fiacre' (70). The count corrects him, saying that it is 'une calèche'. Jo then wakes his brother up with a statement reminiscent of fairy-tale language: 'Dépêche-toi, ta calèche t'attend' (70). Here there is an awareness by Jo of the importance of language in relation to a situation, a deliberate use of fairy-tale language to reassure himself and his brother that everything will end happily ever after.

Such uses of language abound in *Baby-foot*, where the influence of America and the American language are so strong. At the beginning of the work there is the episode where Jo and his friends are discussing *Lucky Strike* cigarettes versus *Camel* ones. Mayer asks Jo in an American accent:

> «Toi aussi, t'est dans le *tobacco*?»
> Il me fait marrer, Mayer, quand il essaie de prendre l'accent américain.
> «Pas tellement, dis-je, je travaillerais plutôt dans le chewing-gum.» (14)

The narration of this conversation strikes as authentically the voice of Jo as a child because of its detail and the comment in the present tense about Mayer's accent. The use of the word 'chewing-gum', presumably not spoken here with an American accent since it is not in the italicised script of 'tobacco', is taken up again a few pages later when Jo swallows a wad of it:

> «Qu'est-ce que t'as, mec? Accouche...
> —Mon chouingom, dis-je, perdant, du coup, mon semblant d'accent yankee (36).

Jo, as a child, also makes the kind of general comment about social and political values that Joffo makes as an adult. As with the comments made above, he couches his comments within the events of the works, relating the issues to his experiences as a child and, frequently, with child-like expression that makes them authentically his actual voice. His comments on the yellow star that he must now wear, are typical:

> Quand on a ça, il n'y a plus grand-chose que l'on peut faire: on n'entre plus dans les cinémas, ni dans les trains, peut-être qu'on n'aura plus le droit de jouer aux billes non plus, peut-être aussi qu'on n'aura plus le droit d'aller à l'école. Ça serait pas mal comme loi raciale, ça. ( 21)

A similar passage occurs when he reflects on the nature of war. This passage is rather more complex in that it starts with the reflections of Jo as a child, using the present tense and child-like syntax, but then shifts into the adult voice as Joffo extends the ideas and the detail of the debate in a more elaborate style. It starts:

> Je suis donc son ennemi?
> On ne s'est jamais vus, je ne lui ai rien fait et il veut me tuer. Ce n'est qu'en cet instant que je comprends un peu maman ou des gens qui venaient au salon à Paris et que j'entendais discuter, ils disaient que la guerre était une chose absurde, stupide et cela ne me paraissait pas juste. (154)

There follows a list of arguments for war not being absurd as he had thought, and then the following sentences, which are clearly those of the adult Joffo:

> Comment pouvait-on dire que tout cela était absurde? Ceux qui le disaient ne comprenaient pas, ils tranchaient, dans leur ignorance, mais la guerre aux yeux de l'enfant que j'étais ne ressemblait en rien au chaos, au désordre, à la police. (154)

### c) Narration and Readership

The issue of narratorship is closely linked to that of readership. Gerald Prince asks why there exists a large body of critical theory on the different types of narrator, but comparatively little on the narratee. He distinguishes between the narratee within a work and the actual reader of it, the former being fictive, the latter being real reader of any time or place. He then proceeds to distinguish between the narratee and the virtual reader, the one for whom the work was written: 'Every author [...] develops his narrative as a function of a certain type of reader whom he bestows with certain qualities, faculties and inclinations according to his opinion of men in general [...] and according to the obligations he feels should be respected.' Such a reader is again different from the 'ideal reader', someone 'who would understand perfectly and would approve entirely the least of his words, the most subtle of his intentions' (*10*, p. 9).

Putting the characteristics of the narratee and readership mentioned above into the context of the two works by Joffo, it is clear that the situation is complex. Joffo explains in his 'Dialogue avec mes lecteurs' that he wrote it for himself as a kind of self-analysis, as a means of exorcising his childhood (**248**). He is the narrator and the initial narratee. But, equally, he says that he wrote it out of a sense of responsibility, putting down on paper what he had told his children (**249**). The children who read the books are the virtual readers whom he had in mind when he was writing them. As children they shift from being the virtual reader to the ideal reader in terms of understanding the childhood experience, but they will not be the perfectly insightful ideal readers in terms of their understanding of the historical and political events. However, as Joffo indicates at the end of his 'Dialogue avec mes lecteurs', he appears to hope that the lessons they learn will make them more insightful, creating a world in which the types of life-threatening dangers he underwent are transformed into a mere game (**253**).

In many ways these works, especially *Un sac de billes* are works about readership, and the importance of constructing meaning through different forms of storytelling. As the reader, whether real or virtual, is presented with versions of reality that have been given some structure or form—i.e. as the reader perceives how a purely chronological sequence of events has been given a perspective, structure and therefore a meaning—, s/he will become increasingly aware of the power of story-telling. By selection of their material and the way they present it, different storytelling structures will have different effects. Some may reveal truth, others may hide it, and the reader will become alerted to the way in which he or she can be manipulated into following another person's way of perceiving the world rather than relying on his or her analysis of it. The effect of storytelling may be positive, but, particularly in the context of World War Two, a period in which the freedom of an individual to decide for him or herself was being denied, Joffo clearly sets out its dangers as well as its benefits.

Storytelling is also closely related to these works as *romans d'éducation,* in particular *Baby-foot,* in that the perspectives they offer can be taken as sets of values in a learning process. A literary work refers to the world outside the work

> ... by selecting certain norms, value systems or 'world-views'. These norms are concepts of reality which help human beings to make sense of the chaos of their experience.[...] Each norm asserts certain values at the expense of others, and each tends to contract the image of human nature to a single principle or perspective. [...] In real life [... the] value systems we encounter are met at random: no author selects and predetermines them and no hero appears in order to test their validity. (*10,* pp. 56-57)

An example of how all these issues work in practice is given by Joffo in *Un sac de billes* when he recounts a story told to him and Maurice as children by his father. One man says to another:

> «Pour que les hommes puissent vivre tranquilles, c'est extrêmement simple, il faut tuer tous les Juifs et tous les cordonniers.»
> «L'autre monsieur le regarde d'un air étonné et au bout d'un moment de réflexion, demande:
> «—Mais pourquoi les cordonniers?

Papa se tut.

Il y eut un silence un peu surpris, maman seule se mit à rire.

Je demandai:

—Mais pourquoi aussi les Juifs?

Papa eut un sourire un peu amer et avant de replonger dans son journal me dit:

—C'est justement la question qui n'est pas venue à l'esprit de ce monsieur et c'est la raison pour laquelle cette histoire est drôle ( **121**).

This story has several levels of narratorship and readership. The narrator is both Joffo as the author of *Un sac de billes* and also the unnamed man who is telling the original story. The 'readers' are the second man, Joffo's father, who first heard the story, Joffo and Maurice as children, and the readers of the book. The story is a selection from the whole set of information of the supposedly real event, the exchange being limited to a short dialogue. This is carefully structured to lead to the question that Jo asks as he reflects on the value judgement or norm that has been presented, demonstrating one person's perspective on the world.

Jo's upbringing in a household accustomed to storytelling makes him very aware of its potential effect. He and Maurice use it to save themselves from danger at the Hôtel Excelsior when they decide to invent a biography for themselves, creating a fictional life in Algiers based on elements of their own lives, but which will avoid suspicion by the Gestapo (**145-6**). Without knowing it, Jo's invented account of how the family never met many Arabs because they lived in separate areas of the city, turns out to be historically plausible (**164**). Their fiction is thus authenticated by evidence. Jo is so skilled in storytelling, that, on another occasion, he is quickly able to fabricate a story about going to Roanne, to prevent suspicion on the station at Cannes (**189**).

In *Baby-foot*, storytelling continues as part of the plot. Much of Chapter Three focuses on Jo's worries about misleading Greenbaum about Étiennette. Greenbaum wants a woman, and trusts Jo to find him one, but Jo knows that the only possibility is this sixty-year-old prostitute, and cannot bring himself to inventing a story about her and introducing Greenbaum to her (**26-33**). Jo, as the potential narrator, is too aware of the effect on his listener. A similar episode based on the sense of trust that Jo inspires in those around him, is seen when Jo and his friends tell Bergolin that he is being eyed by a woman in the bar, and that he ought to ask her to dance. Bergolin asks what the woman is like, and Jo comments: 'Il me demande à moi parce qu'il a davantage confiance. Il a bien tort' (91).

Jo's ability to tell a story causes problems for himself from which he learns lessons about the dangers of storytelling. He lies to his teacher M. Maillard, saying that his father is ill, as an excuse for his lack of attention in class. He realises this time that the fabrication is too unrealistic, a sort of wish-fulfilment based on a dream he has had of his father returning. He admits he has lied, since this time he cannot live with the enormity of the fiction he has created. M. Maillard says that he knew Jo had been lying. Jo, in this case had been a very unreliable narrator (68-71). For Jo, the storytelling episode, rather than affecting the listener, has more of an effect on the narrator. Jo realises that he may now wish to pass his 'certif', if only to be able to show it to his teacher (71).

## Narrative structures based on literature

Jo's storytelling is based on a childhood experience that is grounded in many different forms of storytelling by others, from his father's stories about the family history to the wealth of other forms of narration. These frequently shape the narrative, acting as embedded structures that enable events that are being experienced in reality to be 'read' from the perspective of the original story.

### a) Fairy tales and other literature

As might be expected from a narrative recounted from the point of view of a young child, there are many references to fairy tales. Fairy tales enable the kind of exorcism process that Joffo mentions in his 'Dialogue avec mes lecteurs' (**248**) in that they enable children to undergo life-threatening experiences within a safe environment secure in the knowledge that the ending will usually be a happy one.

Jo refers to fairy tales early in *Un sac de billes* when he describes his reaction to the departure of the SS from the barber's shop: 'Ils devaient déjà être au bout de la rue que nous étions encore figés, pétrifiés, et il me sembla un instant que comme dans les contes une fée maligne nous avait changés en statues de pierre et que jamais nous ne reviendrions à la vie' (**16**). Jo and Maurice's separation from their family and the constant threat of a grim death are elements that recall the children in *Hansel and Gretel or Le Petit Poucet (Tom Thumb)*. Rather like the ogre in *Le Petit Poucet* who threatens to cut up the children and eat them, the Gestapo threaten to cut Jo into pieces if Maurice does not return with the evidence that they are not Jewish (**175**). The old lady who asks them questions on the train to Dax reminds Jo of the ones illustrated in his reading books. He suddenly suspects that he cannot trust her—or indeed anyone—, which recalls the moral lesson by Perrault at the end of his *Petit Chaperon Rouge*, after the wolf, disguised as the grandmother, has eaten Red Riding Hood (**38**). While Jo does not mention the fairy tale by name here, the allusion is clear, though it might be argued that the 'happy end' to the incident recalls other versions based on Grimm, in which Red Riding Hood escapes.

Sometimes it is the language that recalls that of the fairy tale. The words of Henri and Albert when they meet Jo and Maurice: 'Ho, fait-il, ho, ho, voilà les voyous' and 'Ho, ho, a-t-il dit, voilà les voyous' (**87-88**) recall the words of the ogre in Perrault's *Le Petit Poucet:* 'Ah! les voilà, dit-il, nos gaillards', just as Jo's: 'ta calèche t'attend' (**70**) recalls versions of *Cendrillon*. The reference to the fairy godmother of this tale is even clearer in *Baby-foot*, when Jo says: 'Je suis la fée qui change toutes les citrouilles en carrosses et ma baguette est un paquet de dollars' (58).

Both works are full of references to children's and other literature. In his 'Dialogue avec mes lecteurs', Joffo states that he was not afraid to leave his family since he saw himself reliving some of the adventures of the young cartoon hero Bibi Fricotin (**236**).

Bibi Fricotin, created in 1924 by Louis Forton, battled successfully against enemies around the world and even in space. Since Bibi always survived, Jo expected to do so as well. Another interesting reference—made by the farmer with whom Jo and Maurice have spent the night—is to the pseudonymous G. Bruno's *Le Tour de la France par deux enfants* (**66-67**). This was a primary-school textbook published in 1877 which recounts how two children travel through France and encounter all of its glories. As such it was not dissimilar to the sort of propaganda of the French State in World War Two, and had a happy ending. The farmer adds that there were no Germans in the work, thus setting up a contrast between the idealised world of the textbook and reality.

Other works with similar parallels that are integrated into the work are Dumas' *The Count of Monte-Cristo*, when Jo expresses a desire to see the Château d'If (**76**), the setting for the story of the wrongful imprisonment of the hero of the story followed by his escape and the revenge he takes out against those who falsely accused him initially of being a Bonapartist. The parallels here with Jo, assumed to be guilty in a non-Republican state, are clear. Jules Verne's *Michel Strogoff* is also mentioned by Jo (**76**); it is a work that again includes the themes of the long, hard journey and treachery that run parallel to their own situation.

In *Baby-foot*, literature with the themes of the journey and treachery are less important for Jo than literature that focuses on the individual. He sees himself as the heroic d'Artagnan of *Les Trois Mousquetaires* and *Vingt ans après* by Dumas (74-75), and describes himself as being 'fier comme Artaban' (103), a reference to the proud hero of *Cléopâtre*, very similar to d'Artagnan, written by the seventeenth-century writer La Calprenède, though more probably via 'Plus fier que tous les Artabans', a comparison from Rostand's *Cyrano de Bergerac*. However, as noted earlier, the main influences on Jo in *Baby-foot* are not literature, but Hollywood cinema, with its new screen heroes, and the world of boxing, with its sporting heroes.

## b) Mythical and biblical references

Just as Jo has been influenced by the writing of fairy tales, he is also influenced by the mythical stories he has read and the Bible. His adventure is an odyssey, a long journey in search of his home. While the parallels with Homer's epic story the *Odyssey* are not specified, there are many similarities, whether they be in the general search in the *Odyssey* for home and father, or in the detail. There is, for example, the stay with Mme Viale, during which Jo, like Homer's lotus-eating sailors, quickly forgets the world around him:

> Dix jours passèrent ainsi entre les poules, les canards, le mortier, Anatole France et les récits sempiternels de ma chère patronne. Je mangeais fort bien et j'avais oublié la guerre. ( **96** )

The episode with the Compagnons de France recalls Odysseus's stay with Calypso, who fed and clothed him well, and whom he only left when she told him that he must. Similarly Jo's escape from the Gestapo by pretence echoes Odysseus's escape from the Cyclops by trickery. In addition, the *Odyssey* and both of Joffo's works abound in sports, for example boxing and running.

As well as the *Odyssey*, there is the influence of the Bible in relation to Jo's Jewishness. In his 'Dialogue avec mes lecteurs', Joffo writes:

> Je vous dirai maintenant ce que signifie pour moi être juif, en France ou ailleurs, au vingtième siècle. Je pense que c'est être l'héritier d'une grande tradition religieuse qui remonte à Abraham, père des grandes religions monothéistes, à Moïse, le prophète des prophètes, le seul homme qui ait rencontré Dieu, qui l'ait entendu.
> Il en ramena la preuve: les dix commandements. ( **247** ).

Jo and Maurice's journey closely follows that of the Jews in the book of *Exodus*, the second of the five parts of the *Torah* or Pentateuch, coming after *Genesis*. The *Torah* describes the origins of the nation of Israel as a family of herdsmen, their enslavement in Egypt, their liberation and their forty years in the desert, ending with the conquest of the land they will inherit. The book of *Exodus* is central to the *Torah* in that it contains description of the enslavement, the travels and the liberation, thus closely following not only Jo and Maurice's travels across France from a form of enslavement to liberation, but also the travels of Jo's ancestors. It starts with the king of Egypt decreeing that the Israelites are too successful and too numerous. He decrees first enslavement and then the killing of the children. Moses, discovered as a baby, is brought up by Pharoah's daughter—rather like Jo living with the Manceliers—before eventually becoming the leader of the Israelites. Both the book of *Exodus* and the *Torah* end in an open way. At the end of the *Torah*, the Israelites are described as they are about to enter the promised land, just as Jo and Maurice in *Un sac de billes* return to Paris, but we are not told what happens to them.

In addition to the specific structure and narratorship qualities of the *Torah*, there are other biblical references. Just as Peter denies Jesus three times, so Jo has to deny his Jewish faith, firstly to his father, the person who has formed him and given him the rules according to which he must live, like God to Moses with the Ten Commandments (**34**), and secondly to the Gestapo (**159**). Joffo comments on this in his 'Dialogue avec mes lecteurs' when he says that it is obeying a higher principle to remain alive than to claim a belief, if that will lead to death (**242-3**).

Jo is even tempted by a Satan figure. On the train to Dax he falls asleep and dreams that he is being offered lemonade to quench his thirst by Père Boulier. Jo is desperately thirsty and wants to accept his offer, but suddenly he becomes an SS Officer (**40-41**).

## Other narrative structures

As well as the embedded literary references which create narrative structures in the works, there are other significant structuring devices which have an effect on readership. Literature such as the fairy tale takes place out of time, but Joffo's works take place within a chronology. In addition, there are spatial and form-related structures.

## a) Time and history

*Un sac de billes* has various levels of temporal structure, each linked to different aspects of the narrative. There is firstly the chronology of historical events. The novel begins in 1941 and ends with the Liberation of France and Jo's return home in July 1944. Exact dates relating to the progress of the war are given. The most important for Jo, relating to the actual beginning of the end of the war, are given in their fullest form, for example 10 July 1943 (**127**), the date when the Allies landed in Sicily, and 8 July 1944 (**217**) when the Germans left R[umilly], leading to the Liberation of France. Other dates are given less fully, being marked only by the day and month, for example 8 September (1943), the date when Marshal Badoglio signed an armistice at Syracuse, and Italy changed sides (**132**), and 10 September (1943), the date when the SS and Gestapo arrived in Nice (**132**). The year is less significant since the episodes to which they refer are part of the process of the war rather than markers for its beginning or end. Interestingly, the most important date of all as regards the war—6 June 1944, the date of the Allied forces' landing in Normandy—is not given a year (**214**). Jo notes that this day was most significant and dramatic for Mancelier, who by now was no longer listening to the progress of the war on the radio. It thus becomes attached not to Jo, but to Mancelier, as an important date. By leaving out the year there is an implication that Mancelier is cutting himself off from the events of the world around him. A similar effect happens with 8 November 1942, the date when the Allies landed in North Africa. This was a significant marker in the move towards the end of the war, but, as with the 6 June, it is not given a year (**123**). The reason this time is that it is Jo's mother's birthday. The personal attributes accorded to the date are more powerful than the historical attributes as the strength of the family and the family occasion outweigh what is going on around them all.

The effect of the importance of dates, the ways in which they mark events and the relationship between the life of someone and the date, is explored by Jo in relation to 1 April 1944. He has been so taken up in the events of the war and his own survival that, on a date when there is no significant historical development, he forgets that the date is important for other reasons:

> Ça fait le troisième que je rencontre qui rigole derrière mon dos.
> Aurais-je un trou à ma culotte?
> Je passe une main discrète et mes doigts rencontrent le poisson de papier qui me pend depuis le milieu du dos.
> C'est vrai, j'oubliais la date: 1er avril 1944.
> Curieux que les gosses aiment autant faire des farces! La guerre est toujours là, de plus en plus présente, et cela ne les empêche pas de tirer les sonnettes, de suspendre des casseroles aux queues des rares chats survivants qui n'ont pas été transformés en civet. ( 210)

*Baby-foot* has no significant dates relating to contemporary history at all. The dates are all related in some way or other either to Jo's development towards adulthood, as a function of the *roman d'éducation*, or to social life in general. The nearest to a contemporary historical date is at the beginning when he records that it is 1945 and that his father died in an extermination camp during the war (11). He continues to discuss the extermination camps, like the rest of the world at the time. 1945 also means, however, the arrival of chewing gum (36), a very different level of event. Similarly, 1940 is no longer marked as the beginning of the war; Jo sees it as the date when laughter ended (70), while 1939 is marked as the last time a Charlie Chaplin film was shown (19). 1946 is the year in which he obtains his *certificat d'études* (214), and also the year he fails to be Romeo to Bernadette as his Juliette. In fact, the only major historical date given is 1515, the date of the famous victory of François 1er at Marignan. As far as Jo is concerned, it is just another piece of useless information he needs to obtain his 'certif' (14).

### b) Time and the narrator

While it is clear that the progress of time is sometimes given purely chronologically and sometimes in relation to the effect it has on the characters, there is one aspect of *Un sac de billes* in particular in which the chronology is very closely related to the narrator. In his work *When the Grass Was Taller* Richard Coe quotes *Un sac de billes* in relation to the perception by the child of passing time:

> By definition, the Childhood is an extended form, carrying the self from first consciousness to full maturity over an allotted span (normally) of some fifteen to eighteen years. Very occasionally this time-span can be abbreviated for purely internal reasons: because one section of the experience, typically in wartime or revolutionary situations, was so intense that the process of maturation was speeded up to a quite abnormal extent. (*11*, p. 7)

The chronological sequence in *Un sac de billes* is not linear and steady. It speeds up or slows down depending on the experiences being undergone. One episode of extreme speeding-up is is between the end of Chapter X and the opening of Chapter XI (**198-9**). Chapter X ends with a lengthy reflection by Jo on the effects the war has had upon him, how it has hardened him but how he has become indifferent to what is happening, knowing only that he will be able to continue whatever happens. He has been through extreme, abnormal situations, but he is now, perhaps abnormally, able to reflect and think how he is going to leave yet again for further adventures. Just before the end of the chapter he says:

> Demain je serai à Aix-les-Bains. Si cela ne va pas, si un obstacle quelconque surgit, nous irons ailleurs, plus loin, à l'est, à l'ouest, au sud, n'importe où. Cela m'indiffère. Je m'en fous. (**199**)

Jo now believes that he can cope in any circumstances, but his indifference to further dangers may be a form of self-deception. It is the reader who becomes aware of this, accepting Jo's statement of self-confidence and security at the end of Chapter X, but being disorientated by the beginning of the Chapter XI. Between the two is a gap of two months, Chapter XI opening with a description of Jo forging ration tickets while living with the Manceliers in R[umilly]. The reader, who has 'lived with' Jo as he has overcome the dangers and obstacles in his flight across France is disorientated since the chapter does not start with any information regarding time or place. This only comes later. The disorientation brings the reader closer to the absurd world of the war, in which all rational behaviour has disappeared, experiencing at first hand how Jo has felt. The fact that Jo does not appear to notice the gap increases the reader's concern, being forced to ask whether Jo is deceiving himself about his new-found security, or whether he is actually now able to survive, as he had explained, indifferent to what happens.

The Hôtel Excelsior episode of Chapter IX is perhaps the most significant of the episodes with shifts of time, since it includes various types of time sequence. It is the most menacing episode in the work, and abounds in precise detail about the times when events happened, interspersed with different types of time. The chapter starts with a section in which the emphasis in on the apparent normality of life and the slowness of change. A old man is wearing his 'costume des dimanches' and his wife has recently had 'un indéfrisable' (155). They are a couple who have 'vécu ensemble toute leur vie' (156). In this section the indications of time passing are all those of slowness, with the choice of words and expressions such as: 'Au fur et à mesure', 'lenteur', 'lentement' (155-7). Page 157 marks a shift in time once Jo and Maurice are alone. The urgency of the change is given as Jo wonders what time it is and then, a few lines later, notes: 'J'ai envie de faire pipi, cela fait lontgtemps et j'ai peur' (157). From this moment onwards, time speeds up, each detail of the events being noted. There is repetition of such phrases as 'bref échange', 'tout de suite', 'plus vite', 'très vite', and the short exchanges of the examination (157-62). The events pass too quickly and are associated so much with the dangers that Jo is not able to note precise times, only the speed of time. Then, on page 162, he

notes that he has not slept all night and has another interrogation at
6 a.m. The panic and urgency has diminished and he is becoming
more aware of how the terrifying episodes are linked to a precise
chronology. He is losing control over his normal perception of
time, no longer experiencing it as it passes, only perceiving that
certain events occur at certain times. The second day at the Hôtel
Excelsior has an increasing number of gaps, each indicated by the
passing of time, with phrases such as 'Bientôt midi', 'Dans deux
heures je saurai que', and 'Vers sept heures' (**162-5**). By page 166,
the events that are controlling his life have become the norm, and
passing time does not exist:

> Six jours.
>     Six jours qu'ils nous tiennent et ne nous lâchent pas. Il ya eu encore
> un interrogatoire le matin du troisième jour et un autre l'après-midi du
> quatrième. Depuis deux jours, rien. (**166**)

The marking of time returns each time there is a significant
incident, reaching a climax at the end of the episode when they are
so close to being able to leave. The priest has arrived with 'proofs'
of their not being Jewish:

> À midi, il n'avait toujours pas été reçu.
>     À midi cinq, le cure plongea sa main dans une poche profonde de
> sa soutane et en tira un morceau de papier blanc soigneusement plié.
> Le papier contenait deux tranches de pain gris et un morceau de
> mortadelle. [...]
>     Après cet épisode [an ostentatious request for water] il devint
> rapidement l'attraction de l'hôtel, et les responsables comprirent qu'il
> pouvait y avoir là quelque danger, aussi à quatorze heures fut-il
> introduit (**180-1**).

This climax leading to their being allowed to leave is followed on
page 183 by a gap in time as one section ends and another begins:

> Derrière nous, accoudé au parapet, Subinagui nous regarde.
>
> Gérard apparaît à la porte de la cuisine.

Two pages later, the reader learns that the gap is a fortnight long: 'Bientôt quinze jours que nous sommes revenus de l'Excelsior' (185). The reader is not told of what happens in the gap of time. Jo has undergone such an extreme experience in which the detail of every moment was recorded, that he cannot cope with further narration of 'normal' events. He has pushed the episode into his unconscious. The irony is, as he states, that he was put into this extreme situation by time itself. By being arrested on a Friday, the end of the week, a time when the Germans had filled their convoy of people to the detention camps, they were not put onto the convoy and were allowed the time to be able to remain at the Excelsior and obtain the grounds for their release (181-2).

*Baby-foot* is constructed according to a very different time structure. The chapters are separate, each dealing with a different episode in Jo's development. They can be divided into those where the narrative starts in the middle of an event, leading to a narrative which gives the context, and those where there is some indication of the time and context from the outset. Of the first type, chapters I, III, V, VI, XI, XIII and XV are typical. Beween them are the other chapters, setting up a pattern or rhythm that is broadly from one type to the other and back again. The overall impression is of the regularity of life, of one event following another inexorably, and, as Jo explains at the beginning of Chapters IX and XII, almost monotonously: 'Pâques est venu, on a rayé les jours sur le calendrier et ça y est quand même: c'est comme ça qu'on vieillit bêtement, en rayant les jours de notre vie' (86) and: 'Une chose a toujours marqué ma vie: la succession des passions' (132). How different this is from the dynamic interaction with time as seen in *Un sac de billes*. As Jo has grown more mature, his life has become more monotonous. Even those episodes in which time is a major factor, for example in his final fight with Kernadec (122-8), are of a different quality from those in *Un sac de billes*. At the Hôtel Excelsior, time was significant for Jo because the world was out of his control, and his awareness of the different types of time passing were one example of this. In *Baby-foot*, the fight will end whether Jo wins or not; it is a controlled time and he is within it, needing only to fight on until the fight is finished. It might be argued that in the episode when he is waiting on the balcony outside Bernadette's bedroom, time passes in a similar way to that of *Un sac de billes*. Jo is very aware of the time, the fact that he might be on the balcony for several days, but realising that he will be seen by passers-by at day-break (156). However, he eventually falls asleep, and records that he does not know whether he has slept for thirty seconds or three hours (159). This is quite different from the mental blocking mechanisms causing the gaps in the time sequence in *Un sac de billes*.

### c) Spatial structures

The journey from childhood to adolescence and adulthood is paralleled by the physical journey that Jo makes, in particular in *Un sac de billes*. The journey is from Paris, around France and back to Paris, passing through real places which are all identifiable except for R., which Joffo later divulges is Rumilly, near Aix-les-Bains. Each place is associated with an event that is part of Jo's formative experience, whether it be the move forward from Dax where they are helped to escape the S.S. controls, to Hagetmau where they learn that it is possible to lead others across the line, or Nice, where Jo learns the full horror of human nature and is therefore able to be compassionate to M. Mancelier at R[umilly].

The circular movement around France can also be likened to a form of birth, France being the 'womb' in which Jo is to be found at the beginning, symbolised by the strong sense of family that surrounds him. He returns home on his own, able to embark on a life that is continued in *Baby-foot*. It might be argued that this symbolic birth is repeated as a 'rebirth' throughout *Un sac de billes*. Jo frequently finds himself enclosed, whether in the train, the dark forest, a bedroom or interrogation room, and escapes time and time again into the open, undergoing the event of birth many times over. Jo's final train journey appears clearly to evoke a symbolic birth, as he struggles head-first between a pair of legs to find a place, to emerge at last as Jo Joffo:

... je rampe entre deux paires de fesses. Celle de droite ne semble pas
avoir souffert de restrictions. J'incline à gauche. Miracle: un trou entre
deux jambs, je me faufile, je rampe de biais et qui est-ce qui se trouve
au premier rang? C'est Jo Joffo. (**225**)

He has completed an initial stage in becoming an adult, just as the
final line of *Baby-foot* indicates that he has completed the stage of
childhood and adolescent games. He is now able to continue
towards full adulthood, strengthened by the experiences. As he says
in his 'Dialogue avec mes lecteurs':

Et finalement ces quatre années de l'Occupation m'ont apporté une
philosophie. Je me suis par la suite senti bien plus fort pour affronter
la vie de tous les jours, ses pièges, ses échecs, ses deceptions. Pour les
ramener à leurs justes proportions, il me suffisait de me reporter à
cette époque. Et je pense à ce mot de Nietzsche: «Ce qui ne m'a pas
tué m'a rendu plus fort.» (**237**)

# Conclusion

*Un sac de billes* and *Baby-foot* both received an enthusiastic response from readers, who then wanted to know more about the characters' lives before the war. This led Joffo to write a 'prequel', published in 1997. Called *Agates et calots*, it is introduced by a preface in which Joffo explains that he wrote the work in response to his readers' demands. He is clearly very aware, however, that if this were the only function served by the novel, it would not stand in its own right. He states, therefore, that the novel does more than fill in background detail. It serves a didactic or moral function as well, including material about the republican, democratic ideals on which France is founded:

> ... je vais donc, avec votre complicité, vous faire découvrir le bonheur de cette famille dont les parents, immigrés russes, avaient choisi la France, non par le fait du hasard, mais simplement parce qu'il y avait au fronton des mairies trois mots magiques: «Liberté, Égalité, Fraternité». (p. 7)

The novel therefore contains two main elements: detail about Joffo's family and his own life before the adventures of *Un sac de billes*, and general information about the threats to France's republican nature during the period leading up to World War Two. It is set during the three years prior to *Un sac de billes* leading up to World War Two. Jo is seven years old (p. 85), though the stress is not on his age as such, rather on the fact that he is the youngest in the family with three sisters and three brothers, and tends to get spoilt by those around him.

The title refers to two different types of marble, making a specific link to *Un sac de billes*, but the work itself recalls in its form both *Un sac de billes* and *Baby-foot*. It is divided into two main parts and a brief epilogue, the content and the episodic form of *Baby-foot* being reflected in the first part, and *Un sac de billes* being reflected in the second part.

The focus of the first part (pp. 9-153) is on the lessons that Jo learns from his experiences. He learns about social inequality at Freinville where his father buys a 'maison de campagne' (p. 63). The name may sound fictitious, but is not, being that of a company town built in the suburbs of Paris by the Westinghouse Brake Company in 1891. As Joffo explains in the Préface, France is founded on the principles of «Liberté, Égalité, Fraternité» (p. 8), and yet true equality has not been attained. The industrial pollution of suburbs such as Freinville is a marked contrast to the environment of luxury resorts such as Deauville and Trouville. The Joffo family has attained a dream, and indeed it is a magic world for them all, but Joffo is only too aware of the real world of social inequalities that it represents.

Jo also learns personal lessons, for example the dire consequences of getting drunk when given alcohol by his elder brother Albert as a joke. He also learns how to make money by training his dog Woswos to 'accompany' him singing, and by collecting and then selling the scrap metal from the brake factory at Freinville. He learns, particularly from his father's experiences, the dangers of gambling. Perhaps most importantly, he learns about death when he nearly drowns in a swimming pool and, above all, his beloved girlfriend Blanche dies after contracting whooping cough. She was to have accompanied Jo and Maurice to America, a country evoked time and time again by references to Tom Mix and cowboy films, but this dream has to end.

The second part (pp. 155-216) has the circular form and many of the qualities of *Un sac de billes*. It opens with the hopes of the Munich agreement with Hitler in the autumn of 1938. The subsequent invasion of Poland and the declaration of war are also covered. The family, along with many others, is forced to leave Paris for fear of bombing. They go to Brittany where they are initially billeted in luxury at the château of 'Madame la Baronne', as they call her, but are forced to leave once she discovers that they are Jewish. In their second billet, Jo and Maurice are threatened by the local children because they are from Paris. They escape into a forest and are helped by (among many references to fairy tales) a white-bearded giant. The episode has a moral ending as Jo, Maurice and the Breton children learn that not only they, but also people living in Alsace, Auvergne and Corsica, are French.

Once the Armistice is signed, the family returns to Paris where life becomes increasingly difficult for Jews. Henri and Albert are summoned to report for German work camps, the Commissariat général aux questions juives is set up, and the sign «Yiddish Gescheft» is put on the barber's shop (p. 214). All the children apart from Maurice and Jo who are too young, leave for the Unoccupied Zone to escape the growing threat to their lives.

The final comment by Jo in this part is when his mother sews on the yellow star to denote that he is Jewish. He cannot distinguish its form from that of the sheriff's badge that he has seen so many times in American films. This image, in which the real world is fused with that of dreams encapsulates Joffo's overall message. It underpins that of the anecdote at the end of his *Dialogue avec mes lecteurs* in which Jewish and non-Jewish children are able to play together, exchanging roles, and thus freeing themselves of their differences before they become adults. Joffo is a writer whose works cannot be separated from an underlying didactic and moral purpose: to promote the unique sense of freedom that is at the heart of France and which must never be forgotten. As he says in his preface to *Agates et calots*:

> Bien sûr, notre génération attache moins d'importance aux Droits de l'Homme: nous ne savons pas ce que cela signifie d'essayer de survivre lorsqu'ils sont bafoués. C'est très different pour les étrangers qui débarquent dans notre beau pays. «Liberté, Égalité, Fraternité»... Ces mots appartiennent au patrimoine de la France et des Français. C'est unique au monde. J'écris ton nom, Liberté... (pp. 7-8)

# Bibliography

Unless indicated otherwise, works and resources are all published in Paris. The films stated as being available in SECAM format require a multistandard video recorder for full-colour playback.

## Works referred to

1. Maurice Larkin, *France since the Popular Front*, Oxford, Clarendon Press (2nd ed.), 1997.
2. Victor Turner, *The Ritual Process*, New York, Aldine de Gruyter, 1969.
3. Victor Turner, *From Ritual to Theatre*, New York, PAJ Publications, 1982.
4. Ernest Krausz and Gitta Tulea (eds.), *Jewish Survival: the Identity Problem at the Close of the Twentieth Century*, New Brunswick and London, Transaction Publishers, 1998.
5. Isidore Epstein, *The Jewish Way of Life*, London, Edward Goldston, 1946.
6. Johan Huizinga, *Homo Ludens*, London, Routledge and Kegan Paul, 1949.
7. Jacques Ehrmann, Cathy Lewis and Phil Lewis, '*Homo Ludens* revisited', *Yale French Studies*, 41 (1968), 31-57.
8. Isaac Bashevis Singer, *Shosha, a Novel*, New York, Fawcett-Crest, 1978.
9. Mieke Bal, *Narratology: Introduction to the Theory of Narrative* (tr. C. van Boheemen), University of Toronto Press, 1985.
10. Gerald Prince, 'Introduction to the Study of the Narratee', in *Reader-Response Criticism. From Formalism to Post-Structuralism*, ed. Jane P. Tompkins, Baltimore and London, Johns Hopkins University Press, 1980, pp. 7-25.

11. Richard N. Coe, *When the Grass was Taller*, Yale University Press, 1984

12. Northrop Frye, 'The Archetypes of Literature', in *Fables of Identity*, San Diego, CA, Harvest, 1963.

13. Jean-Paul Sartre, *Réflexions sur la question juive*, Gallimard, 1954.

14. Laura Marcus, *Auto/biographical discourses. Theory, Criticism, Practice*, Manchester University Press, 1994.

15. L.A. Renza, 'The Veto of the Imagination: A Theory of Autobiography', in *Autobiography: Essays Theoretical and Critical* (ed. James Olney), Princeton University Press, 1980.

16. Robert Scholes and Robert Kellogg, *The Nature of Narrative*, New York, Oxford University Press, 1966.

17. Leo Bersani, *The Culture of Redemption*, Harvard University Press, 1990.

18. André Malraux, interviewed by Miguel Otero Silva in *El Nacional* (Caracas, Venezuela, 4 August 1945), published in French by *Le Monde diplomatique*, August 1999.

**Other works by Joffo with relevant themes**

1. *Andreï ou le hussard de l'espérance*, Ramsay, 1999. The novel recounts the search for an indentity by Andreï, born to a Jewish mother in the chaotic world of early twentieth-century Eastern Europe as it moves from tsarism to bolchevism. He experiences deportation to Siberia, and escape through Russia, Turkey and the Middle East.

2. *Anna et son orchestre*, Jean-Claude Lattès, 1991. The story of Jo's mother and grandmother, based on the life of Joffo's own mother. A young girl with a 'magical' violin escapes the Odessa pogroms and travels through Europe to safety in Paris.

3. *La Jeune Fille au pair*, Livre de Poche, 1995. First published in 1993. The book focuses on the reasons why a German girl, Wanda, becomes an au pair for a French Jewish family in postwar France.

4.  *Les Aventuriers des nouveaux mondes*, Éditions du Rocher, 2001.
    Joffo's latest novel about adventure and travel, dealing with
    three Jewish pioneers in Palestine and America from 1917 to
    the twenties. In an interview in *L'Alsace* on 31 May 2001, Joffo
    said: 'En 1917, les héros émigrent aux États-Unis. Le roman,
    inspiré d'une histoire vraie, est un voyage dans deux mondes,
    celui des pionniers sionistes et celui de la mafia italienne new-
    yorkaise, et une belle aventure.'

5.  *Simon et l'enfant*, Livre de Poche 'Jeunesse', 1999 [1985]. Set in
    1942, the story tells of how ten-year-old Franck hates his
    Jewish stepfather, Simon. As a Jew, Simon is forced to flee
    Paris, and Franck accompanies him across France. Their
    shared experiences, especially with the *maquis* and in Drancy,
    bring them closer together.

**Other works with relevant themes**

1.  Alain Bosquet, *Les Trente Premières Années*, Livre de Poche. A
    trilogy of autobiographical works (*L'Enfant que tu étais*, *Ni guerre
    ni paix*, *Les Fêtes cruelles*) by an author born in Odessa, living in
    exile after the Bolshevik uprising, firstly in Bulgaria and then in
    Belgium. He saw war service in Europe and North Africa in
    the Belgian, French and US armies.

2.  Claude Gutman, *La Maison vide*, Gallimard, 'Folio Junior', 1993.
    The story of a fifteen-year-old Jewish boy, David, whose
    parents escaped from Poland to France and who is separated
    from them at the *Vel d'Hiv*. He is forced to deny his identity as
    a Jew and return to live alone in his house. *L'Hôtel de retour*
    (Paris, Gallimard, 'Page blanche', 1991), in which David enters
    the Resistance movement, experiences the Liberation and has
    to face up to the fate of his parents.

2.  Art Spiegelman, *Maus*, available in many languages including
    French (Flammarion). A renowned cartoon book in which the
    Jews are represented as mice and the Nazis as cats. A father
    tells his son of his struggle to survive on being sent to
    Auschwitz.

5.   Uri Orlev, *Une île, rue des Oiseaux*, 'Hachette Jeunesse', 1991
     (translated from the Hebrew). The story of an eleven-year-old
     Jewish boy who is left alone with his pet mouse in the Warsaw
     ghetto after his family have been taken away.

**Other relevant resources**

1.   'Discourses of Jewish Identity in Twentieth-Century France',
     *Yale French Studies*, 85 (1994). A very interesting set of articles
     on texts and contexts relevant to both works.
2.   Étienne Fouilloux, *Les Chrétiens français entre crise et Libération
     1937-1947*, Seuil, 1997. A thorough documentation of the
     collusion between the Catholic Church authorities and the
     Germans, and making a distinction between such collusion and
     the help given by many Catholics in France to the Jews.
     Suitable for advanced readers.
2.   Sander Gilman, *Jewish Self-Hatred*, Baltimore, MD, Johns
     Hopkins University Press, 1986. A work that discusses the
     issues surrounding the possibility or not of Jews integrating
     into the society in which they live.
4.   H.R. Kedward, *Occupied France: Collaboration and Resistance 1940-
     1944*, Oxford, Basil Blackwell, 1985. A short, very readable
     work about how ordinary people lived under the Occupation,
     with particular emphasis on the how they reacted to
     collaboration and Resistance.

**Multimedia resources**

The following is a short selection of the hundreds of websites on
Joffo. Search engines, like www.altavista.fr or www.google.co.uk,
will find them. Many have been written as school projects by

students across the world. Their French is not always accurate. They were visited in March 2002, but may since have disappeared.

1.  http://www.accreteil.fr/clgjzaybondy/Lecture/Jeux/jouer.htm. A set of multiple-choice questions in French on *Baby-foot*
2.  http://www.fosf.ch/franzprojekt/franzu1.htm. A Swiss school's site with basic information about *Un sac de billes*, and a crossword.
3.  http://b8.stradax.net/misc/un_sac_de_billes.html. A detailed study of *Un sac de billes* by Beat Strasser.
4.  http://savoirscdi.cndp.fr/Admin/ASP/Biblio.asp?ID=9. An extensive site by the Centre National de Documentation Pédagogique, with a bibliography of fiction in French on World War Two.
5.  http://www.magenta.nl/crosspoint/shoah.html. One of the many websites on the holocaust (Shoah), with many links to other websites.
6.  http://aphgcaen.free.fr/cercle.htm. A very useful website by the Cercle de la Deportation et de la Shoah, with links to articles and other resources on the position of Jews in World War Two.
7.  http://www.charles-de-gaulle.org/dossier/18juin/. A website about 18 June 1940, with newspapers, interviews and a recording of de Gaulle's speech of 22 June 1940.
8.  http://hypo.ge-dip.etat-ge.ch/www/cliotexte/index2.html. A very detailed website on the teaching of history. It is worth scrolling down to the twentieth-century section for texts and chronologies of French history.
9.  http://www2.ac-lille.fr/heg/auschwitz/deport04.htm. A series of pages on anti-Semitism in France in the 1930s and 1940s, with information about the *rafles*, the *Vel d'Hiv*, and concentration camps in France.
10. http://www.histoire.org/2gm/. A fascinating website with much documentation and information. Of particular interest is a collection of propaganda posters to be found by clicking on 'Les Documents' on the homepage and then on 'Notre collection d'affiches'. A poster for the Compagnons de France can be found under the section headed 'Affiches de propagande du gouvernement de Vichy ou des Allemands'.

## Films available on video

1. *Au revoir les enfants*. The celebrated film by Louis Malle in which Jewish children in Occupied France live under false names in a Catholic school. The friendships that develop lead to tragic results.

2. *Lacombe Lucien*. Directed by Louis Malle, this powerful film explores the moral ambiguities of World War Two, as a young French peasant joins the Gestapo, then falls in love with a Jewish girl.

3. *Le Vieil Homme et l'enfant*, directed by Claude Berri. SECAM format, but not available currently. The story of an anti-Semitic Pétain supporter who has to care for a boy, but does not realize that the boy is Jewish.

4. *The Diary of Anne Frank*, directed by George Stevens. The deservedly famous Oscar-winning film of the original.

5. *Un sac de billes*, directed by Jacques Doillon, 1975. Available in SECAM, this version of the novel is disappointing because of the changes made to plot and character. Joffo expresses his own disappointment in his *Dialogue avec mes lecteurs* (**235**).

## CD-ROMs

1. *De Gaulle: un géant dans l'histoire*, INA/Infogrammes.

2. *La Seconde Guerre mondiale + Résistance*, Montparnasse multi-média/Arte.

3. *L'Histoire de la Shoah: de la persécution à l'extermination des Juifs d'Europe*, Centre de Documentation Juive Contemporaine, 37 rue de Turenne, Paris 75003.

4. *Mémoires de la Déportation*, Fondation pour la Mémoire de la Déportation, 71 rue Saint-Dominique, Paris 75007.